James McCosh, Princeton University

Inauguration of James McCosh

As President of the College of New Jersey, Princeton

James McCosh, Princeton University

Inauguration of James McCosh
As President of the College of New Jersey, Princeton

ISBN/EAN: 9783337171346

Printed in Europe, USA, Canada, Australia, Japan

Cover: Foto ©ninafisch / pixelio.de

More available books at **www.hansebooks.com**

INAUGURATION

OF

JAMES McCOSH, D.D., LL.D.,

AS

PRESIDENT OF

THE COLLEGE OF NEW JERSEY,

PRINCETON.

OCTOBER 27, 1868.

NEW YORK:
ROBERT CARTER AND BROTHERS,
No. 530 BROADWAY.
1868.

PREFACE.

At a meeting of the Board of Trustees of the College of New Jersey, at Princeton, April 29th, 1868, the Reverend James McCosh, D.D., LL.D., Professor of Logic and Metaphysics in Queen's College, Belfast, Ireland, was unanimously chosen to the office of President of the College, made vacant by the resignation of the Reverend Dr. Maclean, and a committee was appointed to correspond with Dr. McCosh, and inform him of his election.

On his acceptance of the office, a committee was appointed to make arrangements for the inauguration.

The event, at the same time, called forth unusual marks of public favor on both sides of the Atlantic. In Scotland, as well as Ireland, distinguished assemblies were gathered in honor of the President-elect, to express to him their good wishes at parting. In our own country, the sister Colleges of Harvard, Brown, and Jefferson, conferred upon him their highest academic degrees; and on his arrival at Princeton, October 20th, he was met at the station by the faculties and students of the College and Theological Seminary, welcomed with hearty cheers, and escorted to the President's house, from the porch of which he made a short address to the students, which was warmly applauded.

On the day of the inauguration, October 27th, special trains from New York and Philadelphia brought to Princeton such a concourse of graduates and of learned and distinguished men from different parts of the country, as has never before been known in the history of the College. The procession, which was under the direction of General Caldwell K. Hall, Class of 1857, as Grand Marshal, with Assistant Marshals from other classes, was formed in its several divisions, at Whig and Cliosophic Halls, the Library, Geological Hall, and the Chapel, and at half past twelve o'clock moved towards the First Presbyterian Church in the following order:

GRAFULLA'S BAND.
GRAND MARSHAL.
ORATOR OF THE UNDER-GRADUATES.
UNDER-GRADUATES IN THE ORDER OF CLASSES.
HIS EXCELLENCY THE GOVERNOR AND THE CHANCELLOR OF THE STATE.
EX-PRESIDENT AND PRESIDENT ELECT.
OFFICIATING CLERGY AND ORATORS.
THE BOARD OF TRUSTEES.
THE FACULTY OF THE COLLEGE.
THE DIRECTORS, TRUSTEES, AND FACULTY OF THE THEOLOGICAL SEMINARY.
PRESIDENTS AND PROFESSORS OF OTHER COLLEGES AND SEMINARIES.
JUDGES OF THE UNITED STATES AND STATE COURTS.
MEMBERS OF THE SENATE AND HOUSE OF REPRESENTATIVES OF THE UNITED STATES.
DISTINGUISHED STRANGERS.
ALUMNI AND LAUREATI OF THE COLLEGE.
GRADUATES AND STUDENTS OF OTHER COLLEGES AND SEMINARIES.
CITIZENS.

Arrived at the church, the under-graduates opened in line, with heads uncovered, while the other divisions of the procession passed through them into the church. The Governor and Chancellor of the State, Ex-president and President-elect of the College, officiating clergy and orators, and distinguished visitors took their seats upon the platform at the centre, with the Board of Trustees on the right and the Faculty on the left, while the isles and pews became densely crowded with students and alumni; the galleries having been previously filled with ladies.

The exercises then proceeded according to the order, and with the addresses hereafter presented, being interrupted only by the frequent applause of the audience, which was especially called forth by the appearance upon the platform of the venerable Judge Elbert Herring and Col. Joseph Warren Scott, who received their degrees from President Witherspoon, and by the allusion made to the long and valued services of the retiring President, Dr. Maclean.

The various congratulatory addresses having been delivered, and the oath of office administered, the President then received the College Charter and Keys at the hands of Ex-president Maclean, whose words in connection with the ceremony made the scene peculiarly impressive.

After the Inaugural Address of the President, which was heard with unabated interest to the close, the whole assembly rose and greeted him with enthusiastic cheers.

In the evening the President held a reception at his house, while a promenade concert, provided by the students, was given in the adjoining campus, the College grounds and buildings being brilliantly illuminated.

ORDER OF EXERCISES.

His Excellency, MARCUS L. WARD, Governor of New Jersey, and *ex-officio* President of the Board of Trustees, presiding.

Music.

Invocation.
> By The Rev. JONATHAN F. STEARNS, D.D., a member of the Board of Trustees.

Music, **72d Psalm.**

Address of Welcome on behalf of the Trustees.
> By The Rev. CHARLES HODGE, D.D, LL.D., of the Class of 1815, Professor in the Princeton Theological Seminary, Senior Member of the Board of Trustees.

Address of Welcome on behalf of the Under-Graduates.
> By Mr. J. THOMAS FINLEY, of the Senior Class, representing the Cliosophic and American Whig Societies.

Congratulatory Address to the Alumni and Friends of the College.
> By the Hon. WILLIAM C. ALEXANDER, of the Class of 1824.

Address in Response on behalf of the Alumni.
> By The Honorable JAMES POLLOCK, LL.D., of the Class of 1831, Ex-Governor of Pennsylvania.

The Oaths of Office administered to the President-elect.
> By The Honorable ABRAHAM O. ZABRISKIE, LL.D., of the Class of 1825, Chancellor of New Jersey. The President-elect presented to the Chancellor by The Honorable DANIEL HAINES, of the Class of 1820, and The Honorable CHARLES S. OLDEN, Ex-Governors of New Jersey and Members of the Board of Trustees.

Music, "**Te Deum Laudamus.**"

Delivery of the Charter and Keys of the College to the President.
> By The Reverend JOHN MACLEAN, D.D, LL.D., of the Class of 1816, the retiring President of the College.

Inaugural Address.
> By The Reverend JAMES MCCOSH, D.D., LL.D., President of the College. *Subject:* "Academic Teaching in Europe."

Concluding Prayer.
> By The Reverend GEORGE W. MUSGRAVE, D.D., LLD., a member of the Board of Trustees.

Music, Doxology, **117th Psalm.**

Benediction.
> By The Right-Reverend CHARLES P. MCILVAINE, D.D., D.C.L., of the Class of 1816, Bishop of Ohio.

INTRODUCTORY,

BY GOVERNOR M. L. WARD.

His Excellency, MARCUS L. WARD, Governor of New Jersey, and *ex-officio* President of the Board of Trustees, presided, and introduced the exercises by saying: "This institution of learning, so closely identified with the reputation and honor of our State, is about to install as its President one whose learning, culture, and fame is as wide spread as the language we speak.

"Gifted and able minds have, from the commencement, presided over these halls of learning, and none have been more successful than he, who, full of years and honors, this day resigns the trust to other hands. May he long live to enjoy the esteem of his many friends, and the retrospect of a life well spent.

"From far and wide the Alumni and Friends of the College have gathered to honor the occasion, and to attest their interest in its material progress and its intellectual triumphs.

"Never did its future seem so assured as now—with a faculty first in all departments of knowledge, it stands the peer, if not the superior, of the institutions of learning in the nation."

ADDRESS OF WELCOME

ON BEHALF OF THE BOARD OF TRUSTEES,

BY

THE REVEREND CHARLES HODGE, D.D., LL.D.

REVEREND AND HONORED SIR,—The Trustees of the College of New Jersey tender you their cordial salutations. We regard your accession to the presidency of this institution as a most auspicious event. In no case within our knowledge has an academic election been received with such unmistakable evidence of public approbation. High expectations are entertained of your success in the career on which you are about to enter. Why this is; why such hopes are cherished, it would not be proper for me, in your presence, to state; suffice it to say, that the high positions which you have successfully filled in your own country; the world-wide reputation secured by the productions of your pen; our personal knowledge of you as a Christian gentleman and faithful minister of Christ, are rational grounds for the hope that your presidency will constitute an epoch in the history of Nassau Hall. How these expectations are to be realized, what measures are to be adopted to increase the efficiency and enhance the reputation of the College, we leave to you and your able coadjutors of the Faculty to determine. We would in a single word state what it is we desire. It is that true religion here may be dominant; that a pure gospel may be preached, and taught, and lived; that the students should be made to feel that the eternal is infinitely more important than the temporal, the heavenly than the earthly. We are deeply convinced that all forms of knowledge without religion become Satanic. The ground of this conviction is not the perceived causal relation between impiety and immorality; nor solely the lessons of experience, but the revealed purpose of God, that those who refuse to acknowledge him, he will give up to reprobate mind.

But religion and science are twin daughters of heaven. There is, or there should be, no conflict between them. We earnestly desire, therefore, that all departments of knowledge embraced in the curriculum of such an institution, should be here so cultivated as to secure the highest measure of mental culture, the richest stores of acquired knowledge, and the formation of the best habits for future study and future action.

One sentence more. We earnestly desire that the governing principle in this institution should be love; that the teachers may love the students and the students love their teachers; that these young men may be led by the cords of affection into the ways of order, self-control and diligence.

It is with the confident hope of seeing these ends accomplished we inscribe your honored name to the list of the Presidents of this College. Your predecessors in that office form one of the brightest galaxies in the ecclesiastical and literary firmament of this western hemisphere—beginning with Dickinson, the foremost man in our church, in his generation, and ending with Maclean, than whom no man living among us is regarded with deeper reverence or more sincere affection.

We commend you to the grace of God, and the guidance of our great God and Saviour, Jesus Christ, for whom this College was founded, and to whom it inalienably belongs.

ADDRESS OF WELCOME

ON BEHALF OF THE UNDER-GRADUATES,

BY MR. J. THOMAS FINLEY.
OF THE SENIOR CLASS.

Sol exoptatus illuxit; dies lætissimus festissimusque agitur. Quod bonum, felix faustumque sit, Nassovia venerabilis, colenda semper et culta, præsidem undecimum accipit. Neque nostra solum hujus diei eventus interest, verum etiam ecclesiæ, reipublicæ, seculi.

Curatoribus honoratis visum est nos quoque qui adhuc in gremio Almæ Matris morantur, gratulationes nostras afferre. Ut qui maxime, te ex animo præsidem nostrum salvere jubemus!

Te florem eximium cultus Europæi arbitrati sumus, te scientiæ ac religionis consensus interpretem maximum, te fidei defensorem præcipuum.

Collegii nostri historia tibi haud omnino ignota est. Reipublicæ historiæ vinculis artissimis est intexta. Witherspoon illustrissimus, præses sextus, advena acceptissimus idemque civis tuus, patriæ adoptivæ valde amans, publicis consiliis seculo natali nostro interfuit. Madison clarissimus, ejusdem ætatis alumnus, Reipublicæ præfuit, aliisque muneribus publicis functus est. Ne te morer, ecclesia quoque et theologia sacra præsidibus alumnisque nostris non minus debent. Edwards, Davies, Green, ne alios mortuos viventesve commemorem, famam suam nostramque late protulerunt. In horum munerum honorumque societatem te læti accipimus.

Collegii nostri decus præcipuum fuit, quod artium liberalium studio religio omni tempore præfuerit. Hæc ratio disciplinaris tibi cordi semper fuit, erit semper. Omnem humanitatem commendans et docens, philosophiam veram et religionem præcipue nobis exponas atque exemplo tuo confirmes. "Mater omnium bonarum artium, sapientia," tibi maximam debet gratiam; in ære tuo magis magisque sit. Nihil nobis juvenibus potius est quam ut opera talia tibi bene procedant.

<blockquote>
"Pater ipse colendi
Haud facilem esse viam voluit."
</blockquote>

Utilitas, "justi prope mater et æqui," civibus nostris maximo pretio est. Hac via ardua, utilium sagacissimus nos volentes in sapientiam veram sanctamque ducas!

Patria nostra nondum adulta, mens animusque adolescentes tibi in manus dantur. In bonum verumque nos faciles semper invenias!

Te ipso nobis ignoto, nomen tuum et opera tua haudquaquam ignota sunt. "*Intuitiones*" tuæ hos juvenes instituerunt. Vestigia tua ardentes insecuti sunt. Te cum Kantio, Millio ceterisque luctantem intentis oculis observarunt, et "Habet, habet!" acclamarunt; "Conscientiæ vera philosophia est conformanda." Te vincente verum rectumque triumphantur; nos ergo lætati sumus.

Nobis adventu tuo nihil exoptatius est. Tua salus salus nostra est, fama tua nos quoque illustrat. Labores tui nos omnes in omni liberalium artium studio promovebunt.

Æstate ineunte certiores facti te hæc munera curaturum clamore nostro totum aër implevimus—alis igneis lætitiam nostram in cœlum misimus.

Tibi præsidi nostro honoratissimo omnia beneficia satis superque sint. Nobis te præside favor Dei abunde adsit!

"Appareat beata pleno copia cornu!"

Quum decessor tuus, Maclean, vir veneratus dilectusque semper, tibi muneris insignia dederit, tibi nobisque dignitatem ingrediaris in omnia secula illustrem.

Vivat McCosh! Vivat Nassovia!

Sperantes, fidentes, lætantes te iterum iterumque salvere jubemus.

CONGRATULATORY ADDRESS

TO THE ALUMNI AND FRIENDS OF THE COLLEGE,

BY THE

HONORABLE WILLIAM C. ALEXANDER, LL.D.

BROTHER GRADUATES AND OTHER FRIENDS OF THE COLLEGE OF NEW JERSEY,—It is only within a few days that I have been advised that the duty had been assigned me of tendering to the assembled graduates of the College, and such other friends as have honored us with their presence, the warm and cordial congratulations of the College on its present condition and prospects, and on its good fortune in having at this juncture secured as its President one so capable, honored, and distinguished as the reverend and learned gentleman who is this day to charge himself with the conduct of its affairs. I could have wished that this duty had fallen upon some one better qualified for its suitable and acceptable performance; and now under the embarrassments which surround me, I am even at this moment tempted to shrink from the undertaking of a task which the flattering preference of the guardians of the institution has so kindly and unexpectedly devolved upon me. I am constrained, however, in all my weakness, to enter on that task, and hope to find my strength in the spirit of the cause which animates me. And here, in these circumstances, I may not inappropriately use the words of a distinguished speaker in another land: "Here, where every object springs some sweet association, and the visions of fancy, mellowed as they are by time, rise painted on the eye of memory; here, where the scenes of my childhood remind me how innocent I was, and the graves of my fathers admonish me how pure I should continue; here, standing as I do among my fairest, fondest, earliest sympathies, oh, believe me, warm is the heart that feels, and willing is the tongue that speaks; and yet I cannot by shaping it in my rude and inexpressive phrase, but shock the sensibility of a heart too full to be expressed, and far too eloquent for language." It is an interesting fact, and not without significance, that when the graduates of an ancient College assemble together as we do now, in circumstances of peculiar and unwonted interest, the thoughts of each one immediately revert to the days of his own novitiate. The days of our youth, in every worldly sense our happiest days, come back upon us in such gatherings, and we would fain live over again the hours when we were as yet untainted by the earthy handling of business and of care; and when our models of statesmen and patriots were those stern, impracticable old Greeks and Romans, concerning whom we were accustomed to read with our masters. Such a return of thought is both natural and pleasing, like the coming back of some war-worn soldier, after the vicissitudes of years, to the green quietude of the lap of earth where he had spent his childhood among the hills. Therefore it is that on such occasions our thoughts run back to the days of academic discipline. They were our days of impression. Later traces have been superficial in comparison. Then the seal was set on melted wax, which presently grew hard as rock. What a tribute to the power of academic education! Great men and great scholars have no doubt been made in privacy. But these must forever want the high and almost festive association of joint pursuit, the remembrance of enthusiasm caught from soul to soul in the common race for knowledge and reputation.

There is no literary institution in America around which so many interesting and even romantic memories and associations cluster, as the venerable College in whose behalf we are this day assembled; and the contributions she has made to the cause of the country, of education, and to the church, have never yet been duly recorded and properly estimated and appreciated. Brought into existence at a period anterior to the Revolution, her history during the years of that memorable contest is inseparably interwoven and intertwined with the history of the country. At the breaking out of the Revolution her graduates numbered but four hundred and eighty-three, a large proportion of whom, with many of the students in attendance, passed from her walls to the ranks of the Revolutionary army; and not one single instance can be discovered, after the closest scrutiny, of any one son of the College, during that eventful struggle, having proved recreant or apostate to the cause of liberty and the country, while their blood moistened every battle-field from Quebec to Savannah. If time permitted me (for I am limited in the number of minutes I can occupy) I could point to authentic records in history showing graduates of this College, who, filling the place of humble ministers of the gospel, when the storm of war rolled over the land, assembled together the male members of their congregations, raised a standard of defence, reiterated the old Puritan maxim, that "resistance to tyrants was obedience to God," and placing themselves at the head of their people, were soon found charging at the head of cavalry regiments in front of Savannah, at Guilford Court House, Eutaw Springs, and the Cowpens. (Applause and cheers.) It has been well said that this College literally gave up her staff and stay when her sixth President wended his way to the first Congress in Philadelphia, there to pledge life, fortune, and sacred honor in behalf of the land of his adoption, and at the same time she gave the first fruits of her academic labor when a member of the first class ever graduated affixed his name to the same glorious instrument, the great Magna Charta of our sovereign and separate existence. (Applause and cheers.) From the establishment of the College in 1747, down to the period when America rose "to repel her wrongs and to claim her destinies," and the inhabitants of the thirteen colonies resolved upon the hazardous step of taking a last stand upon the adamantine rock of human rights, God, in his providence, was using this college as an instrument for the preparation of the men who were to perform no unimportant part in that struggle for empire. I have said that the associations which cluster around this College are memorable. I will mention but one or two. There was no darker period in the Revolutionary struggle, none more pregnant with great events and the fate of the country, than that in which Washington made his famous and masterly retreat across *The Jerseys*, closely pursued by the enemy under the command of General Howe, from whom he escaped, by taking a position on the right bank of the Delaware. It was not until, having determined to put all upon the hazard of the die, he had recrossed the Delaware, encountered and defeated the Hessians at Trenton, marched upon and obtained his victory at Princeton, that from within the walls of the then infant College of New Jersey, he was first enabled to give assurance to the world that the cause of liberty was safe. (Applause.) And it is from this spot, where Washington triumphed and where Mercer fell, that this institution continues to diffuse her benign and hallowed influence over the land; and it is upon this ground, rendered sacred by the blood of Mercer, that the sons of the College have assembled from all parts of the country to greet, and welcome, and honor a countryman of that hero and early martyr in the cause of freedom.

In 1783, the Continental Congress, driven by the

enemy from Philadelphia, adjourned to Princeton, and met in the library of the College. The commencement exercises of that year were honored by the presence of General Washington, who sat upon the stage, and was specially addressed by the valedictory orator of his class, himself a soldier of the Revolution, one whose name has within a few years been added to the list of illustrious and departed Presidents of Nassau Hall, and whose mortal remains repose in yonder house of silence.

There have been two remarkable eras in the history of the College. The first was one hundred years ago, in 1768. On the death of Dr. Finley, the president, the trustees, anxious to extend the fame and enlarge the influence and usefulness of the institution, cast their eyes across the Atlantic, and in the person of Dr. John Witherspoon, of Scotland, saw one who was eminently fitted to supply the wants of the institution. They brought him here to preside over the college. He added to European education and great theological and scholastic attainments, a profound knowledge of the science of government. He had a strong sympathy and affection for popular rights, which had been engendered, fostered and cultured in the wars and contests waged by him against the claims of privilege and patronage in his own Church. No man can carefully examine the history of the College and the times without being impressed with the wonderful influence which that extraordinary man exercised on the cause, progress and success of human liberty and the destinies of the country. He seems to have imbued the mind of every pupil with an ardent love of liberty, and to have moulded the minds and characters of the future men of the country, and prepared them for the proud and distinguished part which many of them were destined to perform in the great political drama then about to be enacted. It is a satisfaction for me to observe to-day in the audience several direct descendants of that president of the College; and what is a more extraordinary fact, and more interesting, is, that we have upon this platform two venerable and distinguished men educated under the presidency of Dr. Witherspoon.—(Loud applause and cheers.) They graduated five years before our retiring president was born, and with the frosts of more than ninety winters pressing upon their brows, but with spirits as unquenched, and with a love of their *Alma Mater* as unquenchable, as when, seventy-three years ago they received their first degree at this College, they have this day come up to mingle their congratulations and acclamations with those of their younger brethren, on the accession to the presidency of a distinguished countryman of their illustrious preceptor.

[At this point of Mr. Alexander's remarks the applause was loud and almost impatient, and, anticipating the desire of the audience, gentlemen on the stand assisted to raise Colonel J. Warren Scott, of New Brunswick, and Hon. Elbert Herring, of New York, the two alumni referred to. Their extreme old age and the emotion they exhibited caused the applause and cheers to be renewed, which were continued for nearly a minute. When it had subsided Mr. Alexander resumed :]

The second era in the history of this college is the present. In 1868, one hundred years from the one I have mentioned, the presidency of the College again became vacant by the retiring of that President who for fifty years has devoted all the energies of mind and body, with a zeal unparalleled, to the interests of the institution and to the more enduring interests of the pupils committed to his charge. (Loud cheers and applause.) I have not time, nor is this the place for me to speak of that officer but I will never consent to pass by his name, however casually, in any public assembly, without tendering to him, the friend of my boyhood, the instructor of my youth, the faithful and unwavering friend of my riper years, the homage of my gratitude, warm esteem, profound respect, and most tender affection.—(Prolonged cheers).

The presidency of the college, again becoming vacant, the trustees, animated with the same feeling that governed their predecessors one hundred years ago, desirous to extend the fame and enlarge the influence of the College, again cast their eyes across the same Atlantic to summon to the presidency of the College one, I was going to say of European reputation, but I will say a reputation not confined to countries where the English language is spoken, but extended as far as mental science is known. Indeed his reputation is co-extensive with the scientific world. He has obeyed that summons, and has come among us, and by trustees, faculty, and students, and citizens—the whole population—he has been received with a unanimity and intensity of welcome—with a wild enthusiasm—which it has never before been my lot to witness. And, surely, with regard to that call, we may believe in this case, that the voice of the people will prove to be the voice of God. (Applause and cheers.)

Brother graduates, while we sons of the College are proud of our academic lineage, and consider that the position of president of the College is inferior in point of honor and responsibility to none other in the land, yet remember that in accepting the call, and in obeying your summons, your new president has severed ties of no ordinary character—ties which bound him to the land of his nativity, to his kindred, to the scenes of his childhood, youth, education, and subsequent usefulness, to the graves of his fathers, and to scenes endeared by a crowd of gentle and attractive associations. He has come a stranger to form new ties and new acquaintances and friendships. What claim has he not to the sympathy, countenance, support, co-operation, and prayers of every son of this College? Remember that it was only when Aaron and Hur held up the sinking hands of the greatest ruler and lawgiver the world ever saw, that the armies of Israel prevailed against the hosts of Amalek. Let your prayers then be that the God of our fathers—that covenant God who for more than a century has blessed this institution, may still continue to guide, and protect, and bless, and send down increased blessings upon her incoming president. (Applause.)

I have strange visions of the future career and grandeur of this College—strange feelings, emotions, and anticipations, as looking down through the long avenue of time, I in imagination see the dawn of a more brilliant day, and feel and believe that the light which even now illumines the path before us will prove to be the precursor of a brighter glory. These feelings, as I stand before you, I have been endeavoring to chastise—to suppress and drive back the emotions and anticipations which have poured in upon me like a flood, and almost incapacitated me for the performance of the duty which I have, perhaps unwisely and weakly, undertaken. That duty is now performed; and it only remains for me to say, in regard to this college under this new administration, may her former glory be equalled and excelled! May the zeal of her guardians and the fidelity of her instructors know no abatement; the affection, devotion and loyalty of her sons suffer no diminution; and amid the numberless literary institutions now scattered throughout the length and breadth of this great confederacy, may no classic steeple point more proudly to the skies than the much loved spire of our own Nassau Hall!

ADDRESS

ON BEHALF OF THE ALUMNI,

BY THE HON. JAMES POLLOCK, LL. D.

GENTLEMEN ALUMNI AND FRIENDS OF THE COLLEGE OF NEW JERSEY.—In the midst of the cares of professional life, literature and leisure are almost forgotten terms—memories of the past, not present realizations. Therefore it is that the duty of this hour becomes almost oppressive. But the inspiration of the occasion relieves the oppression, and bids the lips utter what the heart feels.

I have been requested to respond in the name of the alumni and friends of the College to the address of congratulation to which we have listened with so much pleasure. The duty assigned is at once personal and representative: personal, in the expression of my feelings and sentiments on this inauguration day; representative, in declaring the continued friendship and devotion of the alumni to their Alma Mater, and pledging, in their name, and may I not add by their authority? their cordial, active, and earnest co-operation in maintaining the past renown and speeding the coming day of her greater efficiency and glory. Her honor is their honor, and we rejoice with her in hailing the advent of one whose name is the pledge of progress and reform—whose fame is the synonym of intellectual triumph, and who, filled with the enthusiasm of humanity, and the love of God, is prepared to meet the demands of the age and act in harmony with the mighty movements of the present.

Therefore, honored sir, in the name of the alumni of this College, we bid you welcome to the classic shades of Princeton; to the high office to which you have been called; to our country, our hearts, and homes. In the name of a common ancestry, language, and literature; of kindred and hallowed memories; of truth triumphant over error, terror and death; of an open Bible, a common Christianity, a free church, free schools, free thought, and free speech, we welcome you. You come at an auspicious time in our national history. The rush and roll of war have ceased in our land. The "confused noise of the battle of the warrior" is no longer heard, and "the garments rolled in blood" are no longer seen. Our nation, rising with renewed strength from her late struggle, and wiping the drops of her bloody baptism from her brow, stands before the world redeemed from the stain of human slavery. Liberty and peace, in happy union, are gathering in their trophies, and pointing with gratitude and pride to a more glorious future.

The future of America! What shall it be? You are now with us and of us, to mould and form that future. You come from the land of the Bible and the Covenant, the land of the martyr and the hero, and shall we fear to entrust to your care and guidance the youth of

America, those who are our life, our hope, our future? Oh, no! The Bible of the Mayflower was Scotland's Bible, and it is the Bible of America—the bulwark of her liberties—the power and strength of her nationality. Your Bible is our Bible, and your God our God—therefore we will not fear. How necessary this when we remember that our Government is the embodiment of the power of a free people in the simple forms of our social and political order—that American nationality is the correlative of American manhood—its development and type; that sovereignty is with the citizen, and the supreme and ultimate power of the State is in the ballot-box, vitalized and energized by free, intelligent, and impartial suffrage.

How important that our literary institutions should be controlled by sanctified intellect—that the church and the school-house, twin sisters of civilization and religion, should be seen dotting our valleys and crowning our hills, that the "common school-house," the centre and power of our educational system, "the people's colleges," should be found everywhere in our land, with doors wide open, inviting all to enter upon whom God has enstamped the sign and signet of manhood!

In the Republic of Letters there is no dwarfing selfishness, no partisanship, no sectionalism, no sectarianism. All is cosmopolitan, liberal, universal. In other years Scotland recognized this truth, and gave Witherspoon to America.

Again America has asked, and McCosh is ours. In

asking, we honored Scotland; and in giving, Scotland honored herself and America. She gave us the "type" of her own true manhood, the representative of her intellectual power and advancing civilization. We, with the blood of nations in our veins; as a nation, the epitome of the world's nationalities, by the magic of our free institutions will give McCosh and freedom to the world.

In the land from which you come nobility is hereditary—the recognized law of social, civil, and political life. Birth and blood make and mark the man, affix the title, and determine his position in society. Here nobility finds its title and illustration in virtuous action, in grand achievement, in intellectual power and moral worth. Here we recognize the nobility of honored and honorable succession; and we recognize you, sir, as the honored successor of a band of historic and immortal men, noblemen, upon whose brow God himself affixed the seal of true nobility, of manhood in its full development and impressive grandeur—a succession more honorable and more enduring in its fame than any recorded in the volumes of heraldry or created by royal decree. Need I name your illustrious predecessors in the high office to which you are called: Dickinson, Burr, Edwards, Davies, Finley, Witherspoon, Smith, and others, now among the honored dead, or he who is with us now, the true-hearted, the generous and sympathetic friend, the scholar and the man, President McLean, who to-day so gracefully lays aside the robes of office, and retires with the "God bless him" of all the alumni and friends of the College. These all were men of giant intellect, of positive faith, of lofty patriotism, undying energy and devoted service to country, humanity, and God. The alumni, now associating the past with the present, and recognizing in our new president a teacher and scholar worthy of such honored association, accept the congratulations offered, and seal them with the pledge of renewed devotion to their Alma Mater—her interest, her honor, and renown.

It is also a matter of congratulation, that whilst the president elect comes to us in all the freshness of vigorous manhood; in the fullness and strength of a cultivated and matured intellect, he has brought with him a *heart* warm and true to all the generous sympathies of humanity; that can hold companionship with intellect; that can soften the stern dignity of official position, and blend in harmony the gentle and severe; unite without compromise, the president of the College with the guardian, companion, and friend of the students; a heart that can meet the heart of the young, feel its responsive throbs, and then, with the magic touch of hand to hand, true as the heart, cause him to feel his manhood, and love the one that rules by love; a power greater than official authority; the secret and centre of true administrative ability. The recognition of a student, by friendly greeting from president and professor, the honest shake of his hand, with a heart in it, is a power in the government of a College greater than bolts or bars, bye-laws or tutors, reprimand or expulsions. This *heart power* will govern our Alma Mater.

We are standing to-day in the midst of thronging and touching memories. The past—solemn in its silence, impressive in its history—attends us here. The present—with its living, rushing energies, its "audacious activities"—is ours, and bids us onward. The future—rich in events that await the development of coming years—grand in its relations to the present and the past, takes up the word "onward," and points significantly from the known to the unknown, to be revealed in mightier achievement than the past can boast.

Mind moves, as does the world. We live not in an ideal age, but in an age of ideas—of grand progressive thought, developing the practical and the real, the spiritual and the free. Thus while science and art, with wondrous energy, despite ocean depths, tie with the electric wire continents together; science, literature, and Christianity, with mightier power, binds heart to heart, and nation to nation, and while thrones are trembling and sceptres falling from the hands of profligate rulers, speed the day when earth's empires, united under the banner of the Cross, shall acknowledge the brotherhood of man, and God, the Father of all, as the "King of kings, and Lord of lords." Again, in the name of the alumni, we accept the congratulations tendered, renew our pledge, and pass over to history the doings of this hour.

DELIVERY OF CHARTER AND KEYS.

After the oaths of office had been administered by the Hon. ABRAHAM O. ZABRISKIE, Chancellor of the State of New Jersey, the Reverend John Maclean, D.D., LL.D., the retiring President, delivered to the President the Charter, Laws, and Keys of the College, with the following remarks:

Mr. PRESIDENT,—In the name of the Trustees of the College of New Jersey, and by their authority, I deliver to you the Keys of this institution, the original Charter, and also copies of the Charter as amended, and of the Laws. The obvious design of this ceremony is to declare publicly, by a significant act, as well as in words, that you are fully invested with all the powers, privileges, and prerogatives which pertain to the President of the College; and that in the discharge of your official duties, you are to take the Charter and the Laws of the College for your authority and guide.

While it is the duty of the President to see that the students are properly instructed in the several departments of knowledge embraced in the prescribed course, and that the rules of the College are duly regarded by all concerned, it is more especially incumbent upon him to have the oversight of the religious instruction, to guard the morals of the students and their faith in Christ. For these the laws make him personally responsible; and in so doing, they accord fully with the aim of the pious and excellent men who laid the foundation of the College, and sought thereby to promote the cause of our blessed Redeemer, and the welfare of our race, by the erection of an institution for the advancement of true religion and sound learning.

In the instruction and government of the College, you will have able and learned colleagues, upon whose hearty co-operation you may confidently rely, and who will gladly aid you in securing for the youth committed to your care a thorough, liberal, and Christian education.

It is our earnest and fervent prayer that, in discharging the duties of your great and important trust, you may ever have the guidance and aid of the Holy Spirit, and that your administration of the affairs of the College may be marked with signal ability and success. At such success, no one will rejoice more than your immediate predecessor in office, who bids you welcome to this scene of your future and of his past labors.

INAUGURAL ADDRESS.

ACADEMIC TEACHING IN EUROPE.

How does it come that, with so many superior men in America, I have been invited to become President of Princeton, is a question which I have often been putting to myself these last few months, without being able to find a satisfactory answer. So I think it best to "give it up," and turn to inquiries which have no personal bearing.

But before doing so, I feel bound to say that the very fact of your calling me to this high office is a proof that you have no jealousy of the old country. It is one of the motives impelling me to tear myself from the land which I so much loved, and to come to this country, which I will not love the less because I loved and do still love the one I have left, that I may labor to bring the two nations on which the future welfare and progress of the world do so much depend, into warmer friendship, and closer fellowship. Are we not one in race, a somewhat mixed race, the main element in both being the Anglo-Saxon with its love of personal liberty and its perseverance; the same in language, in literature, in religion, in the love of education and of freedom? Why, with such bonds uniting them, should not the hearts of the two great communities beat in unison, and their hands combine in common efforts for the Christianization, the enlightenment and civilization of mankind. I do not expect to be able to further this end by politics (in which I do not mean to appear as a partisan); but surely all here may help it by the binding influence of literature, science and philosophy, which are citizens not of one country but of the world; and above all by the attractive power of religion, which is a citizen of heaven come down to spread peace among men.

The question for me to answer is, what can I do for you now that I am among you? The reply to this question in all its width must be found in what I do the remainder of my life. But there is a narrower and more immediate inquiry, what can I do this day in response to the generous reception you have given me? All that I can offer is to give some information derived from the experience through which I have passed.

It so happens that I have a considerable acquaintance with the universities of the old world. I have attended two of the Scottish Universities, and I believe I am a graduate of three of them. I have visited Oxford and Cambridge, and lived within their walls with some of their most distinguished men. In Ireland I was officially connected with the latest established university in the Three Kingdoms, the Queen's University; and I had incidentally means of being acquainted with Dublin University. I have visited some half dozen colleges in Germany and several in

Switzerland and Holland. I feel therefore that I ought to know something of academic teaching in Europe. And then it also happens that the question of what academic education ought to be, is being keenly discussed in Germany and in England, Scotland and Ireland by some of the most thoughtful men in those countries, such as Dœllinger, Pattison, Mathew Arnold, Seeley, Farrar, Lowe, Grant Duff, J. S. Mill, Tyndall, H. Spencer, Huxley, Lorimer, Cairnes, and many others. The younger moving spirits in the old colleges are alive to the evils which have become encrusted round the venerable structures to which they are attached, and are bent on having them removed. The more enlightened teachers in Oxford and Cambridge are becoming ashamed of the exclusive study of Latin and Greek, or Mathematics, very specially of their exaction of verse-making—as Milton expressed it long ago: "Themes and verses wrung from poor striplings like blood out of the nose, or the plucking of untimely fruit." In Scotland they have become fully aware of the futility of imparting erudition by mere lectures, and have introduced more of the tutorial and examination system.* Even in

---

* But there is a risk that certain dispensers of patronage, by preferring candidates trained at the English Universities, most of whom have abandoned Presbyterianism, bring the Colleges into collision with the religious convictions of the people. There is another danger: by aping Oxford and Cambridge, without equalling them in their own line; and by glorying in the fact, that their best pupils leave them to get prizes at the English Universities, they may lose that independence of thought and scientific research for which the Scottish Colleges have been famous. There are Englishmen who see

Germany some are becoming sick of their drill system and dry routine, and are longing for an infusion of the more fresh and manly training of Great Britain. This discontent with the present is stirring up a strong desire to improve for the future: and out of the discussions will arise, I am satisfied, great improvements in the Universities of the old world. I am in this lecture to carry you into the very heart of these discussions.

It is to be understood that in doing this I have no design, avowed or secret, to revolutionize your American colleges or to reconstruct them after a European model. I take up this subject because it is one competent to me, and because it enables me to unfold what I believe to be the proper nature of collegiate instruction, without committing myself prematurely to American questions, in regard to which I am seeking information. It fortunately so happens that I have also visited upward of a dozen colleges and theological seminaries in the United States; and I have seen enough of them to become convinced that they are not rashly to be meddled with. They are the spontaneous outgrowth of your position and your

---

this. Professor Seeley says: "If we take the single department of philosophy, is it not evident that if the English system had been followed in the Scottish Universities, there would have been no Scotch school of philosophy." Mr. Johnson: "It is to Edinburgh men more than to any public school or Oxford or Cambridge men (unless Oxford and Westminster take credit for Bentham), that we owe the enlightened legislators and the righteous government of the last forty years." "If we ever had an educator, it was Dugald Stewart."—See *Essays on Liberal Education*, pp. 117, 353.

intelligence; they are associated with your history and have become adjusted to your wants; and whatever improvements they admit of must be built on the old foundation. Still the circumstance that you have called me from a foreign country is a proof that you are anxious to receive supposed good from any and from every quarter. A composite nation like yours, drawing its population from all regions, will be ready to take knowledge from all lands. In regard to elementary schools Europe has more need to look to you than you have to look to Europe: but possibly in regard to universities America may advantageously look to the old colleges of Europe, even as these are anxiously looking to each other. This is one of the European wars in which I would have the United States to take their part. I certainly do not ask you to adopt any European method because it is European, or on any other ground than that it can stand a sifting examination on its own merits: and of this I am sure that whatever matter your country receives from others, it will put upon it, as it has done upon the divers people who have come within its wide territories, a stamp and a character of its own.

I. WHAT IS THE IDEA OR FINAL CAUSE OF UNIVERSITY TEACHING?

On this point, which settles every other, there is no agreement theoretically or practically. A large and growing number, we may call them the realists, evidently think that the τέλος, or end of a university, is to impart knowledge, some would say mere physical knowledge; to fit students for the professions, or prepare them for the business of life. Others, whom we may call the idealists, embracing the more elevated minds, deem this a low and unworthy aim for the highest educational institutions of a country to set before them; and maintain that it should be the ambition of a university to improve the faculties of the mind, to refine the taste, and to elevate the country by raising up an educated body of men, who draw up all who are under their influence to a higher level, where they will breathe a purer atmosphere. Let us endeavor to cut a clear path through the thicket of this controversy.

(1.) I do hold it to be the highest end of a university to *educate;* that is, draw out and improve the faculties which God has given. Our Creator, no doubt, means all things in our world to be perfect in the end: but he has not made them perfect; he has left room for growth and progress; and it is a task laid on his intelligent creatures to be fellow-workers with him in finishing that work which he has left incomplete, merely that they may have honorable employment in completing it. Education ought to be a gymnastic to all our powers, not overlooking those of the body; that every muscle may be braced to its manly use; that our students may be able to assume the natural posture, and make proper use of their arms and limbs, which so many of our best scholars feel, in their public appearances, to be inconvenient appendages. It should seek specially to stimulate, and strengthen by exercising, the intellectual powers: such as the generalizing or classifying, by which we arrange the things that present themselves into groups, ordinate and co-ordinate; and the abstracting, analyzing capacities by which we reduce the complexities that meet us to a few comprehensible and manageable elements; and the reasoning faculty by which we rise from the known and the present to the unknown and remote. The studies of a university should be organized towards this end, and all its apparatus of languages, sciences, physical and mental, and mathematical exercises, should be means to accomplish it. But then man has other endowments than the understanding, in the narrow sense of the term: he has a fancy capable of presenting brighter pictures than any reality; an imagination which will not be confined within the limits of time and this world; and a taste and sensibility which can appreciate beauty and sublimity in earth and sky; and these ought to be called forth and cultivated in our academic groves, by youth being made to know, and led to relish, our finest literature, ancient and modern, in prose and poetry,—I add, though in doing so, I may seem to be placing the ideal too high, by having in museums and art galleries the means of displaying the esthetic qualities of the creature, inanimate and animate, in art and nature. It is a favorite idea of Sir Charles Bell's, that the ancient Greeks reached such incomparable excellence in their statuary by aiming to produce figures as far removed from the brute form as possible : certainly it should be the aim of academic teaching to give a form to the mind high above the brute shape—high above the sordid and earthly manifestations of humanity. And surely our universities, which are to fashion the ruling minds of the country, are never to forget that man has high emotional susceptibilities which should be evoked by narratives, by eloquence, by incidents presented in history, in literature, and in art; and that, as the crown upon his brow placed there by his Maker, he has a moral and spiritual nature, which is to be developed and purified by the contemplation of a holy law, and of a holy God embodying that law, and of a God incarnate and with creature sympathies, inducing us to draw nigh when otherwise we should be driven back by a consciousness of guilt on the one hand, and a view of the dazzling purity of the Fountain of Light on the other.

Now, at this entrance examination, every study seeking admission into the curriculum of a college should be made to appear. In order to matriculation, it must show that it is fitted to refine and purify the noble faculties which God has given us.

(2.) Under this, it should be the aim of a university to impart knowledge. I say *under this,* in order to impose the proper limit on the principle held by so many in the present day, that a college should give itself mainly, not to languages, and least of all dead languages; not to metaphysical pursuits, which move in circles without advancing; not to such old studies which are leading a sort of doomed existence, like that of flies in autumn; but to real knowledge, to practical knowledge, by which it turns out that they mean the various branches of physics, or quite as likely one or two favorite departments of natural science. Now I hold that even for practical utility, for mere happiness' sake, there may be a higher end than the attainment of knowledge, and that is the improving of those heaven-bestowed powers which acquire knowledge, but acquire many other things of value; I maintain that there may be other knowledge valuable as well as scientific information; and I utterly deny that the acquisition of knowledge, certainly not of the material world, is the only means of training the nobler parts of humanity. The child prefers nursery rhymes and Robinson Crusoe to science made easy. Some of the greatest minds that shine as stars above our world knew little of physical science, such as Homer, and Socrates, and Plato, and Dante, and Shakespeare, and Milton, and Edwards, and Burke, and Wordsworth, and Schiller, who yet found in our world sources of high enjoyment and a means of ascending to their elevated spheres. I hold that there are other means besides the natural sciences of educating even the faculties of comparison and causality: that these may be called into exercise quite as effectively by the thoughts and sentiments embodied in a cultivated language; by the study of the noblest part of God's workmanship in this lower world, the human mind, whether of its laws, as unfolded by mental science, or in the concrete exhibition of human nature, in its fears and hopes, its joys and sorrows, its struggles and its triumphs, in countries remote and near, in ages past and present, as detailed in travel, in history, and biography, or by representations in poetry, in eloquence, in the fine arts, and most truthfully of all, in the inspired records.

But then it should be frankly acknowledged and publicly proclaimed, that science, that is, observational science, that the knowledge of nature, that is, of the works of God, is an important means of cultivating those powers with which the God of nature has endowed us; for they show us how to observe and how to arrange the objects with which we are surrounded, and as we do so, we come to see properties and beauties before overlooked, and become more interested in them, and acquire a friendship for them. They show us how to gather the law from the scattered particulars that present themselves; how, by the necessary "rejections and exclusions," as Bacon says, to draw out the essential from the indifferent;

how to reach the truth and consistency among discordant and apparently contradictory appearances; when to lay aside prepossessions and anticipations; and how to make an "inquisition" of nature, to catch her when Proteus-like she is anxious to escape, and make her reveal her secrets. These are not only the true means of acquiring knowledge, but the fittest for exercising and giving energy to the faculties, and of acquiring intellectual habits of patience and penetration, useful in every kind of inquiry, speculative and practical. The old schoolmaster adage, that it is of no consequence what the faculties be employed about, provided they are employed, and thereby disciplined, is a false one. Some have gone so far as to say, that no matter whether the knowledge thus acquired, say the writing of Latin verses, be of any use in the future life or no; no matter how dull and crabbed the work, how harsh the grindstone on which the mind is ground, provided thereby the faculties are sharpened for use. These persons do not see that the mental powers are not healthily exercised, and are not likely to be invigorated and refreshed when engaged in unprofitable work, as it were, mounting the steps of a treadmill, or doing the whole in a close medieval atmosphere, which, in fact wastes the strength, and gives a sallow complexion to the countenance. Do you not see the terrible risk of wearying and disgusting the mind, when it is making its first and most hopeful efforts, and giving it ever after, by the laws of mental association, a distaste for severe studies?

True, the exercise of the mind, like that of the body, is its own reward; but both are most apt to be undertaken when there is some otherwise pleasant or profitable object in view, and most likely to be repeated when we have a sense of gratitude for the good we have received. If, after we have walked so hard, we see and find nothing of value, if we are required to labor for that which profiteth not, to fight as one that beateth the air, the issue is not likely to be refreshing, and life, and hope, but ennui, and unconquerable aversion to exertion. I hold that every study should, as far as possible, leave not a distaste, but a relish on the palate of the young, so that they may be inclined to return to it.* However it may have been in the dark, or rather, as I would call them, the twilight ages, when only a few departments of real knowledge could be discerned, and men had to make the best of the available material, it is not imperative now to resort to profitless studies when such rich and fertile fields are evidently lying all around us. Our Lord's test applied to religion admits of an application to study, namely, that it brings forth fruits. Faith may often be more valuable than works, but it is by works

---

* Plato says, *Rep.* VII. 15, that instruction should be so given that it may be learned without compulsion. Τί δή; Ὅτι, ἦν δ'ἐγώ, οὐδὲν μάθημα μετὰ δουλείας τὸν ἐλεύθερον χρὴ μανθάνειν. οἱ μὲν γὰρ τοῦ σώματος πόνοι βίᾳ πονούμενοι χεῖρον οὐδὲν τὸ σῶμα ἀπεργάζονται, ψυχῇ δὲ βίαιον οὐδὲν ἔμμονον μάθημα. Ἀληθῆ, ἔφη. Μὴ τοίνυν βίᾳ, εἶπον, ὦ ἀρίστη, τοὺς παῖδας ἐν τοῖς μαθήμασιν ἀλλὰ παίζοντας τρέφε. Some of his statements go too far. Quinctilian's caution is judicious: Nam id in primis cavere oportebit, ne studia qui amare nondum potest oderit, et amaritudinem semel perceptam etiam ultra rudes annos reformidat.

it is to be tried to see if it is genuine, and by works
faith is made perfect: so it is by profitable work that
the faculties are called forth and elevated. Bacon
adopted our Lord's distinction, and applied it to science; not holding (as those who do not understand
religion misunderstand him) that practical fruits are
better than knowledge, but that knowledge cannot
be genuine when it does not yield such fruits. So,
using the same distinction, I hold that in study, while
the true end is the elevation of the faculties, they
never will be improved by what is in itself useless, or
found to be profitless in the future life. And I am
prepared to show that the sciences, physical and
moral, not only supply nutriment and strength to the
intellect, they give life to it. It has been proved by
recent science, that the food we eat, got from the
animal and the plant, not only gives nourishment to
the frame, but by the force derived from that great
source of force, the sun, furnishes the heat which
keeps the body warm and vital; so knowledge, which
is power derived from the Divine source of all power,
not only communicates strength to the mind, but imparts fire to kindle a noble enthusiasm, and motive to
set us forth in our pursuits, when we know that we
shall in no wise lose our reward. Science discloses
not only a utility, but a beauty in objects which, to
the vulgar, appear dull and debasing; shows that
there is a loveliness in every work that God has
made, even in the skeleton of rattling bones, from
which the uninitiated shrink; even in the insect

crawling in the clay from which they flee—a beauty fitted to call forth admiration and love, and in the hearts of the pious adoration and praise.

(3.) It may be the aim of a University to give professional instruction. This, indeed, should always be esteemed a lower end, not indeed an unworthy, but still an inferior end, that is, subordinate to the improvement of the mind; and if we make it supreme, we are turning things upside down, and putting uppermost the limbs, instead of the head which ought to subordinate and guide the whole. It is certainly not the function of a University to make its students artizans, or merchants, or manufacturers, or farmers, or shipowners; the practical knowledge required by such may best be got from practical men in shops, and fields, and warerooms, and offices. Still, as science aids art and perfects it, so a College by teaching the sciences may fit its students, not, it may be, for the ordinary avocations of their employments, but for inventing new instruments, and finding improvements; and, by its whole training, it lays up enjoyments denied to the uneducated. But, in order to accomplish even such ends as these, a College should never come down from its high position to be a mere instructor in the mechanical arts, or in shop and office work. Whatever branches it teaches, it should teach as sciences, and in a literary academic spirit, so as to impart to those members of those professions, who come within our precincts, a thoroughly scientific acquaintance with their subjects, so that they may improve the trades and increase their resources, while they carry with them an elevation of tone which will keep the meanest work in which they require to engage from being felt to be a degradation. And then there are walks of life, such as the learned professions, those preparing for which require to know literature and science, and certainly to these the instruction given should be of a philosophic character, to fit them for entering in an intelligent manner, and with a rich furniture of fundamental and established principles, upon their professional studies. But the different branches admitted into the University being so taught, it may be allowable for the student to give a preference to those which may assist him in his professional pursuits. Thus, those who are intended for theology, might legitimately and properly show a partiality for the language of the New Testament, or for mental science which brings them into such intimate connection with the great truths of religion; and a medical student might draw lovingly towards chemistry or physiology; while the lawyer might give less attention to other subjects, to undertake a more special study of political economy. All this is in entire harmony with the idea of a University, whose office it is to train the powers, but which may do so by any thing which is fitted to elevate and refine the mind.

(4.) It should be the aim of a University to promote literature and science, and by these and by its pupils to raise the whole community. The Rev. Mr. Pattison of Oxford would have his University look on the teaching vocation as a subordinate one, and devote its splendid revenues to make its Colleges houses for a "professional class of learned and scientific men;" "homes for the life study of the highest and most abstruse parts of knowledge." This is carrying an idea, which has some truth in it, too far. I am not sure that the healthiest scholarship or the highest science would be promoted by the men who might be selected, no matter on what principle of candidature and election, to these offices of leisure and emolument, which would tend, I fear, to become places of ease and laziness, possibly of obstruction to activity and independence of thought; or whether the men would best accomplish the end by being formed into an exclusive community. Of this I am sure, that the people of this country and of every country will insist on its Universities being primarily the educators of its more promising youths, destined for the higher walks of life. Still those who are placed in the offices of a University should aim at something more than being merely the teachers of a restricted body of young men. The youths who are under them and who look up to them will be greatly stimulated to study by the very circumstance that their professor is a man of wide sympathies and connections with the literature or science of the country generally, or of other countries. It was thus that the Scottish professors of last century, such as Adam Smith, and Reid, and Stewart, and Black, and Munro, and Playfair, did so much to promote their favorite departments, in political economy and mental philosophy, and certain branches of physics. It was thus that Newton, Lucasian Professor of Mathematics at Cambridge, published the *Principia*, and made his University and his College famous for all time. It is thus that in our day in Germany every professor labors to bring forth every year or two the product of his studies in a work which may add to the permanent knowledge of mankind in some department, wide or narrow. The applications of science and the good uses of literature may be found elsewhere in our workshops, and schools, and lighter literature, but where should we expect to find our highest scholarship and profoundest science but in our Colleges with their leisure, their independence, and the great stimulus which they furnish.

And then the glory of every Alma Mater consists in her children, "as arrows in the hand of a mighty man;" "happy is he, that hath his quiver full of them; they shall not be ashamed, but they shall speak with the enemies in the gate." It should the ambition of every College to send forth a body of educated men who, as ministers, as lawyers, as physicians, as private gentlemen, or in the public service, or as engaged in business which their character and refinements elevate, are spreading around them, consciously or unconsciously, a civilizing and humanizing influence : making learning respected because respectable, and spreading a thirst for culture. Such a radiating power is especially needed in our day, when there is such devotedness to the practical and money-making pursuits—to what Sir W. Hamilton translating a German phrase, calls the "bread and butter sciences;" and we need it to counteract the coarseness, the earthliness, the clayeyness, thus engendered, and to set before the country higher and more generous ends. God shows in all his works that he sets a value not only on bare utility but on beauty and ornament,—you see it in that lily so adorned, in that dome of heaven spangled with stars. I suppose that in this country your coal and iron, your earth and oil, are after all more valuable than your precious metals, but since God hath deposited them in your soil you would not part with your silver and your gold. So you should see that with all your other attainments, with your general intelligence and your eminence in the practical arts, you have also the highest learning and science. Our Colleges in relation to the lower education should rise like towers and steeples out of our towns and villages, like hills and mountains out of our plains. A College like Princeton should, as Athens and Alexandria were in ancient times, be an intellectual metropolis whence a refining influence goes down to the provinces. I magnify mine office: a professor should be like the central sun with planets circulating around it, and each of these a centre round which other bodies revolve; so a professor by himself and by his pupils and their labors may reach in his influence to the most distant hamlet in the country through which his students are scattered.

II. WHAT SHOULD BE THE BRANCHES TAUGHT?

Should they be many or few? Should they be the old or new, or both? These are the vague questions put, and the answers have been as vague. Let us seek to clear the way.

I am prepared to vindicate the high place which has hitherto been allotted to languages in all the famous Colleges of the Old World and the New; though I cannot defend the exclusive place which has been given them in some. Without entering upon the psychological question whether the power of thinking by means of symbols be or be not an original faculty of the mind; or the physiological one, whether its seat, as M. Broca thinks he has proven, be in the left hemisphere of the brain, specially in the posterior part of the third frontal convolution of the left anterior lobe, I am prepared to maintain that it is a natural gift, early appearing and strong in youth. You see it in the young child acquiring its language so spontaneously, and delighting to ring its vocables the live-long day; in the boy of nine or ten years of age, learning Latin—when he could not master a science—quite as quickly as the man of mature age. Now, in the systematic training of the mind, we should not set ourselves against, but rather fall in with this natural tendency and facility. Boys can acquire a language when they are not able to wrestle with any other severe study; and why should they not be employed in what they are capable of doing? There are persons for ever telling us that children should be taught to attend to "things," rather than "words." But then words are "things," having an important place in our bodily organization and mental structure, in both of which the power of speech is one of the things that raise us above the brutes. And then it can be shown that it is mainly by language that we come to get a knowledge of things. This arises not merely from the circumstance that we get by far the greater part of our knowledge from our fellow-men through speech and writing, but because it is, in a great measure, by words that we are induced, nay compelled, to observe, to compare, to abstract, to analyze, to classify, to reason. How little can we know of things without language? How little do deaf mutes know of things till they are taught the use of signs? I have known some of them considerably advanced in life who not only did not know that the soul was immortal, they did know that the body was mortal. Children obtain by far the larger part of their information from parents, brothers, sisters, nurses, teachers, companions, and fellow-men and women in general, and this comes by language. But this is, after all, the least part: it is in understanding and using intelligently words and sentences that children are first taught to notice things and their properties, to discern their differences and perceive their resemblances. Nature presents us only with particulars, which, as Plato remarked long ago, are infinite, and therefore confusing, and the language formed by our forefathers, and inherited by us, puts them into intelligible groups for us. Nature shows us only concretes, that is, objects with their varied qualities, that is, with complexities beyond the penetration of children, and language makes them intelligible by separating the parts, and calling attention to common qualities. Nouns, verbs, adjectives, conjunctions, and other parts of speech in a cultivated tongue, introduce us to things, as men have thought about them in the use of their faculties, and combined them for general and for special purposes; primarily, no doubt, for their own use and advantage, but turning out to be a valuable inheritance to their children, who get access to things with the thought of ages superinduced upon them—as it were, set in a frame-work for us, that we may study them more easily. In the phrases of a civilized tongue, we have a set of discriminations and comparisons spontaneously fashioned by our ancestors, often more fresh and subtle, always more immediately and practically useful, than those of the most advanced science. Then a new language introduces us to new generalizations and new abstractions, made, it may be, by a people of a different genius and differently situated, and thus widens and varies our view of things, and saves us from being the slaves of the words of our own tongue, saves us, in fact, from putting words for things, putting counters for money (as Hobbes says), which we should be apt to do, if we knew only one word for the thing. Charles V. uttered a deep truth, whether he understood it or no, when he said that a man was as many times a man as he acquired a new tongue. Then, in learning a language grammatically, whether our own or another, we have to learn or gather rules, and judiciously apply them, to see the rule in the example and collect the rule out of the example; and in all this the more rudimentary intellectual powers, not only the memory, but the apprehension and quickness of perception and discernment are as quite effectually called forth and disciplined, as by any other study in which the youthful mind is capacitated to engage.

I have been struggling to give expression in a few sentences to thoughts which it would require a whole lecture fully to unfold. Such considerations seem to me to prove that we should continue to give to language an important—I have not said an exclusive—place in the younger collegiate classes. Among languages a choice must be made, and there are three which have such claims that every student should be instructed in them; and there are others which have claims on those who have special aptitudes and destinations in life. There is the Latin, important in itself, and from the part which it has played. It has an educational value from the breadth, regularity and logical accuracy of its structure, giving us a fine specimen of grammar, from its clear expression, and from its stately methodical march—like that of a Roman army. It is of inestimable value from its literature, second only to that of Greece in the old world, and to that of England and Germany in modern times;

and a model still to be looked to by English and by Germans, if they would make progress as they have hitherto done. Then, besides its intrinsic worth, it has historical value as the mother of several other European languages, as the Italian, the French, the Spanish, and Portuguese, to all of which it is the best introduction, and, as one of the venerated grandmothers of our own, ready to tell us of its descent, its lineage and its history; let us not forget, as the transmitter of ancient and eastern learning to modern times and western countries; and as the common language for ages in literature, philosophy, law and theology, and thus containing treasures to which every educated man requires some time or other to have access. Then there is the Greek, the most subtle, delicate and expressive of all old languages, embodying the fresh thoughts of the most intellectual people of the ancient world, and containing a literature which is unsurpassed, perhaps not equalled, for the loveliness, purity and grace of its poetry, for the combined firmness and flexibility of its prose, as seen, for instance, in Plato, who can mount to the highest sublimities and go down to the lowest familiarities without falling—like the elephant's trunk, equally fitted to tear an oak or lift a straw. And it is never to be forgotten, that it is the language of the New Testament; that it was the favorite language of the Reformers. Luther said, "If we do not keep up the tongues, we will not keep up the gospel;" and so the stream is still to be encouraged to flow on, if we would keep up the connection between Christianity and its fountain. A nation studiously giving up its attention to these tongues would be virtually cut off from the past, and would be apt to become stagnant like a pool, into which no streams flow, and from which none issue, instead of a lake receiving pure waters from above, and giving them out below. These languages differ widely from ours, but just because they so do, they serve a good purpose, letting us into a different order and style of thought, less analytic, more synthetic, as it is commonly said, more concrete, as I express it; that is, introducing us to things as they are, and in their natural connection. True, they are *dead* languages, but then, just because they are so, we can get a completed biography of them; and, as we dissect them, they lie passive, like bodies under the knife of the anatomist. As Hobbes expresses it, " they have put off flesh and blood to put on immortality;" they are dead, and yet they live; live in the works which have been written in them with their diversity of knowledge, living specially in their literature, which is imperishable, which, for fitness of phraseology, brevity, clearness, directness, severity, are models for all ages, bringing us back to simplicity, when we should err by extravagance; and to be specially studied by the rising generation in our time, when there is so much of looseness and inflation, stump oratory and sensationalism. It would be difficult to define it, but we all know what is meant by a *classical taste;* there are persons who seem to acquire its chaste color spontaneously, as the ancient Greeks and Romans must have done; but, in fact, it has been mainly fostered by living and breathing in the atmosphere of ancient Greece and Rome; and our youths may acquire it most readily by travelling to the same region where the air is ever pure and fresh. I believe that our language and literature will run a great risk of hopelessly degenerating, if we are not ever restrained and corrected, while we are enlivened and refreshed, by looking to these faultless models.

There are other foreign languages which have a claim on educated men, such as the French with its delicate conversational idiom, and the abstract clearness, amounting to transparency, of its prose; and the German with its profound common sense, and its noble literature, worthy of being placed alongside that of ancient Greece, and excelling it in the revelation of the depths of human nature. I am inclined to the opinion that either of these might under certain restrictions have a place in the Course, provided always it be taught as Greek and Latin are, that is, as branches of learning, taught philologically, taught so as to illustrate character and history, and above all so as to open up to us, and lead us to appreciate, the literature of the countries.

But prior to all these and posterior to them, above them all and below them all, is a tongue which has an imperative claim on us; and that is, our own tongue, the language of the mother of us all, Great Britain and her colonies, and the language of her eldest daughter, which should acknowledge her inferiority only in this, that she is the daughter and the other the mother. It has a claim on our love and esteem because it is our own tongue which we learned on our mother's knees, the tongue with which we are and ever must be most familiar; because it is in itself a noble language, with roots simple and concrete striking deep into home and heart experience, and grafted on these from foreign stocks abstract terms for reflective and scientific use; because it has been enriched by the ideas and fancies, the comparisons and metaphors, of men profound in thought and fertile in imagination; and yet more because of its manly and massive, its rich and varied, literature, prose and poetic, revolving round themes which it never entered into the heart of Greek or Roman to conceive. If a Briton or an American can study only one language let it be the English. A College youth's education is incomplete, though he should know all other tongues, if he be ignorant of the genius and literature of his own. There should, I hold, be a special class for the English language and literature in every College of every English-speaking country. But in order that English have a place in a University it must fall in with the spirit of the place and conform to its laws: it must be taught as a branch of learning, as a branch of science (wissenschaftlich); it must be traced up to the roots; it must be studied in its formation, growth and historical development; and, above all, it must be taught so as to give a relish for its noblest works, and secure that it has a literature in the future not unworthy of the literature of the past.

(2.) Mathematics should also constitute an essential part of a College curriculum, and a portion should be obligatory on every student. Over the gates of every College should be written what is said to have been inscribed over the Academy in which Plato taught, "Let no one who is without geometry enter here." They serve ends which can not be effected by any other training. First, they introduce youths early and conveniently to self-evident truth. They show that every thing cannot be proven: that there is such a thing as *a priori* principles founded in the very nature of things, and perceived at once by intuitive reason,—it was to mathematics that the great German metaphysician primarily appealed in establishing the existence of necessary truth. This is a very important conviction to have fixed in the minds of young men, especially in these times, when an attempt is made to derive all certainty from experience, which must ever be limited, and can never—any more than a stream can rise above its fountain—establish a universal, a necessary proposition. Having seen that there are *a priori* truths in mathematics the mind will be better prepared to admit that there are eternal and unchangeable principles lying at the basis of morality and religion, and guaranteeing to us the immutable character of the law and of the justice of God. Then mathematics exhibit to us more clearly than any other science the interdependence and connections of all truth, and the links by which premises and conclusion are tied in the reasoning process. Moreover the study gives a concentration to the attention and a logical consecutiveness to the thoughts, and so saves from that tendency to wandering and dissipation of mind, which is the ruin intellectually of thousands. "For if the wit be too dull they sharpen it, if too wandering they fix it, if too inherent in sense they abstract it" (*Bacon*). It furnishes the fittest discipline to brace the mind for hard intellectual work, and has been found, in fact, an admirable training for those professions, such as law, in which force, tenacity and close application are required. These advantages are altogether independent of the value of the science as an instrument of deduction and a verification of discovery in so many departments of natural science; a use which will be seen to admit of ever widening application as it comes to be determined that every department of physical nature is regulated by form and quantity, the qualities which mathematical science claims as its own rich possession. Not only so, but as it was found long ago that geometry rules beauty addressed to the ear, that is music, so I believe it will be ascertained, as science advances, that it reigns in the beauty of form and color addressed to the eye; and so there is a grand truth in the old Platonic idea that God geometrizes: He geometrizes in all the order and all the loveliness we see in the universe. The withdrawal of a mathematical training from a College would be equivalent—to what God has absolutely prevented his creatures from doing in the universe—to the withdrawal of *force*, and would leave the institution enfeebled and without the power which binds the whole.

But can there be a thorough education of the mind merely by classics and mathematics, as the famous Cambridge system supposes? I hold that these may be taught and learned in the most perfect manner, and yet a large number of the noblest faculties of the mind left uncalled forth, and therefore uncultivated. Mixed with them there should be branches which require students to be more than intelligent recipients, which demand of them that they put forth independent thought and observation.

(3.) The physical sciences should have a place in a full-orbed system. These were not born when universities were established, and resistance has been offered to their introduction on the part of the superstitious supporters of the old, especially the narrow partisans of classics. But they have established such claims on the attention, they have been so "frugiferous" as Bacon anticipated, that it is now certain, whoever may oppose, that they must in the future have a large place allowed them: and if uncompromising resistance is continued much longer the stream will so rise as to break down the dam that would oppose it, and sweep away the good which should be retained with the evil that should be abandoned. So it is expedient in every way to allow a legitimate outlet to these flowing, I will add fertilizing, waters.

There are certain of our natural faculties which cannot be evoked and cultivated so effectively in any other way as being employed about the works which God has made. From an early period youth should be taught how to use and thereby educate the senses, how to observe and how to gather and treasure up facts. And physical science is an instrument not merely for educating the senses; it calls forth all the faculties which discover relations. The facts fall under the senses, but the law which we are ever striving to reach, the law, which binds the facts, can be discovered and comprehended only by the higher intellectual powers, which divide and combine and infer. As it is out of the scattered and isolated parts that we have to collect the law, τὸ ἕν ἐν πολλοῖς, so the study gives a discernment and a shrewdness to the mind, admirably preparing it for taking its part in the tangled affairs of life. It is one of its special advantages that it gives the bracing activity of the chase as well as the triumph of the capture: it not only yields results, it requires us to look at the processes by which these are reached; it not only gives information, but, what is equally important, it teaches us to investigate; it not only imparts knowledge, but prepares us to acquire more by showing us how to make an inquisition of nature; it not only furnishes fruit, but brings us to the tree where the fruit grows and where we may continue plucking: thus even when taught by a skillful teacher it has many of the advantages of self-education.

These sciences are now becoming very numerous and very varied. They may be divided in a variety of ways according to the end we have in view: but for our educational purposes they fall into two classes according to the capacities they incite and educate. One of these groups has been called the Classificatory by Dr. Whewell: it proceeds on the idea that this world is a *mundus*, is a κόσμος, that there is a heaven-appointed order in nature which man can discover, an arrangement with due ordination and subordination in respect of such qualities as form, color, time, and quantity, which it should be our business to seize, and distribute the innumerable plants and animals into kingdoms, and orders, and classes, and genera, and species, and varieties. The other group aims rather at finding internal properties and causes, and may pass under the general name of Physics, embracing such branches as chemistry and natural philosophy, in which we seek to penetrate into the constitution of things and go back from what presents itself to what has produced it. Both groups require more than the receptive and reproductive faculties: the one requires us to discover resemblances and analogies, the other calls forth the powers of analysis and causality. The former depends more on observation proper, the latter proceeds more by experiment and tries by torturing nature, without paining her, to make her disclose her secret machinery. Both are inductive in their nature. Geology combines the two; proceeding on classification so far as it looks to organic remains, but from effects now visible rising to causes working many ages ago, and showing that our earth has had a wonderful history. These sciences begin by the gathering of facts, and would thence rise to the law of the facts, hoping always in the end, when they have discovered the law, to descend by deduction to the foreknowledge and prediction of phenomena. They demand and exercise very varied mental powers and are thus profitable, altogether independent of their practical fruits, which are so palpably beneficent that they allure many to the study who would never be led by the mere love of knowledge.

(4.) It will not be expected of one who has devoted so much attention to the Mental Sciences, that he should overlook them or the contiguous Social Sciences, in speaking of the subjects which should have a place in a College curriculum. I am prepared to show, in spite of the scoffs of some of the votaries of physical science, that there are true mental sciences, such as Psychology, Logic, Ethics, and let me add Metaphysics, the science of first principles, and Asthetics, or what I call Kalology, the science of beauty and sublimity; that they disclose to us laws of great scientific beauty and practical value: that the study of them is fitted at once to whet the acumen and widen the horizon of the mind; and that it is of vast importance in the present day to save us from that, I will not say gross, but subtle materialism which is at the spring-tide in England, in France, and among certain classes in Germany. We have an immediate means of knowing mind just as we have a direct means of knowing matter: we have an inward sense as well as outward senses, if we know matter by sight, touch, taste, smell and hearing, we know the varied operations of mind in knowing and feeling by self consciousness. It is possible then to observe the facts of mind: in our own minds directly, and in other minds by the expression of their inward states in their words and acts; and it is possible to analyze and classify the phenomena, and reach laws as settled as those of natural science. This has been done with more or less success by many, beginning with Aristotle, but has been accomplished with special success by the Scottish school, such as Reid, Stewart and Hamilton.

Now, I hold that the pursuit after the fugitive facts of mind, the seizing of them under their various disguises, the discovery and the expression of the exact laws, such as those of the senses, association, memory, imagination, comparison, reasoning, the tracing of them in our own mind and those of others, furnish exercises of subtle analysis and grasping synthesis, and lead us to distinguish the things that differ, and to perceive profound and remote analogies, in a way and to an extent which cannot be matched by any other study. So much for psychology: and then we have the old mental sciences, which have had a great degree of certainty since the days of Aristotle. Thus we have Logic unfolding the laws of thought, in apprehending, judging, and reasoning generally, especially as employed in weighing evidence and reaching truth; giving rules to which the ultimate appeal must be made in all doubtful matter, and supplying a police to detect fallacies. Then there are Ethics, unfolding the laws of our motive and moral nature, of the emotions, the conscience and the will, showing how man is swayed in motive and in action, bringing us face to face with an eternal law guarded by a holy Governor, and coming down practically to the responsibilities and the daily experience of life. Scotland and Germany have got much elevation of thought from continuing to give these departments a high place in their Universities; though the latter has so far counteracted this by long running after a wild idealism, which, in these late years, has produced a reaction towards a materialistic empiricism. It is a grand defect in the two great English Universities, that they have not given an avowed place to the inductive study of the mind. True, Cambridge has always had moral philosophy, but it has been jostled into a corner by other studies, especially mathematics. Oxford has given a place to formal logic and to philosophy generally, but the latter has come in by a side door, by the school of *literæ humaniores*, where it appears in an examination on the Republic of Plato or the Ethics of Aristotle, and takes the form of the history of philosophy, an important branch, when philosophy itself, that is, the inductive science of the human mind, has previously been taught, but without this, keeping as far from the human mind as classics or mathematics. I believe that the present evil tendencies in these two Universities, a sickly attachment to ritualism among the weakly devout, and a rush to Comtism and materialism among another class, embracing a large number of the aspiring tutors and students, have sprung very much from the neglect of the philosophy of consciousness so fitted to generate an independence of thinking and a comprehensiveness of vision. I am glad to find that the mental sciences, and these taught in a sound, that is, inductive manner, with a constant appeal to the facts of our nature, have a fair place in the American Colleges; and within the sphere of my influence, it will be my endeavor to sustain and defend them.

Closely allied to the purely mental sciences are some others, which consider mankind in their social relations, and are, therefore, called Social Sciences, such as political economy, jurisprudence, international law, and history, considered as a branch of science, and not a mere collection of narratives. I can speak only of one of these, and that is political economy, the science which treats of the accumulation and distribution of national wealth. The inquiry calls forth some of the most useful powers of the mind, such as that of finding unity and law in complexities; of arguing the true causes from mixed effects; and of foreseeing consequences in very perplexing circumstances. It also furnishes a fine example of the joint inductive and deductive methods. It has a special importance in a nation like this, where the government is in the hands of so many, and where it is of such moment to create an intelligent public sentiment, and where wrong economical views would issue in such wide-spread mischief. The study is surely of very particular value to all who are to guide public opinion by the press. The periodical literature, which exercises such influence in this country, will never be elevated till those who supply it have, as a rule, a College education in the principles of political science.

Now I hold that, in a University, *Studium Generale*, there should be representatives at least of each of this fourfold division of subjects. And if our years were as many as those of the antediluvians, or as long as those of the planet Jupiter, I would be inclined to enjoin all of them on every student. But the father of medicine has told us Ὁ βίος βραχὺς ἡ δὲ τέχνη μακρή, and an attempt to enforce all in a course of four years would, at best, secure a smattering of all, without a real knowledge of any, and your *magister artium* would be a "jack of all trades and a master of none." I say, if you are to admit, as you must in justice as well as in expediency, the new branches without excluding the old, then you must allow a choice. All should be in the University, open to all; but all should not be compulsory on each. The question then arises, and I believe it to be the most practical and pressing of all, with whom should the selection lie? With the

University, that is, the governing body? or with the students? My answer is, with both.

It should be so far ruled by the University, as to secure that all the branches be taught academically, taught scientifically, and that, in order to the Master's Degree, every student should go through an enlarged course—a course calling forth the various faculties, and embracing representatives of the four groups, languages, mathematics with applications, physical and mental science. I am prepared to maintain that a University should not give an unrestricted choice to one claiming the literary and scientific degree; if this were done, the student would be tempted to take the easiest subject and the least profitable because so easy; or adhere to the one he had first learned; or confine himself to the one for which he had a taste; whereas, the object of a higher education should be to call forth all the faculties, and widen the sphere of vision. In Germany, where each student chooses his own programme, I believe evils have arisen from the unlimited license; though these are lessened by the circumstance, that he has commonly a defined professional examination before him. There is a great risk in these times of minds of great power and strong tastes, becoming very narrow in some respects, and altogether misshapen, by the exclusive culture of certain faculties to the neglect of others. We see the fisher with broad chest and brawny arms, but with small thin limbs, because the rowing has expanded one part of the frame and allowed the other to shrink;

so we find great classicists, and great physicists, and great mathematicians, and great metaphysicians, weaker than others, when taken out of their own magic circle, in fact, silly and childish, and despising every other department of knowledge. If there are evils in sectarianism in religion, there are like evils in a scientific partisanship; if it is wrong to divide the body of Christ, it is equally improper to divide the body of science, in which all the members are so intimately connected with each other, that no one has a right to say to its neighbor, I have no need of thee. It should be one of the aims of a University to correct this one-sidedness of mind, which is infinitely more unhealthy than any mal-development of the body. It is to be counteracted by requiring every student to have such an acquaintance with each of the grand groups as to know the elements, to have an idea of its method, and to be able to appreciate its importance.

But keeping within this limit prescribed by the final cause of a University, there may surely be a choice allowed the student. In these days, when the circle of knowledge is so widened, the days of universal scholars is seen to be gone by, and if any one pretends to have mastered *omne scibile*, he must be a mere book-worm, if he is not a coxcomb, or a pedant dull as a dictionary. A selection, then, must be made, and this may surely be partly left to the student; he may sometimes go wrong, but far more frequently he will be led aright by irrepressible, inborn instinct.

As all have not the same intellectual stature, it is unnatural to force all to stretch on the same Procrustes' bed; and, if you attempt it, you will only cripple the mental frame. All are not born with the same aptitudes and tastes; and the same reasons which induce us to cultivate our natural talents should lead us to encourage, foster, and develop special genius, when God has bestowed it. Any youth of ordinary capacity may learn elementary mathematics, and will be profited by it; but I defy you even, "with a pitchfork," to make every one a great mathematician, or to force a taste for the study. Every educated man should know classics till he can read any ordinary work, and enjoy the literature of the great authors; but I would not have him drilled thus the whole years of his course, provided he has shown meanwhile a decided taste for other studies. How often have we found the youth, sick of dead languages and abstract formulæ, feeling an inexpressible sense of relief, and as if a new life were imparted to him, when he is allowed to turn to the contemplation of the beauties of nature, or the wonders of the human mind.

I am inclined to think that, in the early years of College attendance, there should be an introduction to representatives of the principal branches of learning and knowledge. I am convinced that these might be so taught as to furnish a gratification, a pleasure, *guadia severa*, to the student, by the variety of food presented. I have heard it argued that the horse was not so soon wearied in old times, when he had to go up hill and down dale alternately, and had thus a change in the muscles exercised, than he now is, when the strain is on the same muscles from morning to night on our leveled roads. However this may be, it is certain that a student, when wearied of one subject, feels himself refreshed when allowed to turn to another requiring a different set of powers. With an introduction in the first two years or so to varied representative branches, I would allow considerable divergences, were it only to avoid a workhouse uniformity of dress and exercise, in the third and fourth years; nay, I would allow time for peculiar studies, and even miscellaneous reading, at least in vacation time. You see I would not have a choice made till there has been an introduction to all the groups; for, until the student has entered a department, and gone a certain length, how can he know whether he has a taste for it or no; how can he know whether he has an aptitude for geometry till he has gone over the books of Euclid. Supposing a boy to begin Latin at the age of nine or ten, I hold that by seventeen or eighteen, he might have a general acquaintance with, and an appreciative recognition of the value of, the various departments of useful knowledge; and then, within the wide bounds prescribed by the College, I would set him free to follow the bent of his nature wherever it may carry him.

The question is often discussed whether it is better to have a general knowledge of various subjects, or a thorough acquaintance with one? You see how I would decide the question. In these days, when all the forces are seen to be correlated, and all the sciences to be connected, I would have every educated man acquire a broad, general acquaintance with a number and a variety of branches, and I would have this followed up by a devoted study of a few or of one. To use a distinction which I met with the other day in reading James Melvill's Diary, let education first be "circumferential," then "centrical." This, I believe, is following the course of nature, which, as every physiologist knows, begins with the general, and then develops into the special. Thus far I would encourage πολυμαθεια, that it may lead us to μιαμαθεια. I would first allow the energies to disperse, as from the sun, and then I would collect them into a focus, as by a lens. In this way I would seek to combine width of view with concentrated energy. Let the student first be taken, as it were, to an eminence, whence he may behold the whole country, with its connected hills, vales, and streams lying below him, and then be encouraged to dive down into some special place, seen and selected from the height, that he may linger in it, and explore it minutely and thoroughly.

III.—IN WHAT MODE SHOULD THE SUBJECTS BE TAUGHT?

By professors or by tutors? by lectures or dry text-books? In Oxford, in Cambridge, and in Dublin, the teaching is chiefly by tutors giving instruction to pupils one by one, or in small companies. In Germany, in Scotland, and the Queen's Colleges, Ireland, the teaching is by lectures delivered by professors, accompanied in the two last by class examinations, more or less formal. In Scotland there were professors, both last century and this, who did little more than deliver lectures, often very brilliant and stimulating, and fitted to rouse susceptible minds, which often felt satisfied but without being filled with any thing solid. There has been a reaction against this extreme, and now considerable attention is paid to examinations; and tutors are employed to assist the professors, and in most cases a text-book is employed.

The question is keenly discussed, which of these methods is the preferable? I hold, on the one hand, that lectures serve most important ends. True, they may not give more information than a text-book, but they bring the living lecturer into immediate contact with the living pupils. There is great advantage, also, in having the students in companies, that is, in classes, and these considerably large ones. This arises not so much from mere emulation, that *calcar industriæ*, of which the great Jesuit schools made so much use, as from the heads and hearts being made to beat in unison—as even two time-pieces going at different rates will come to do when placed on the same wall; it arises from the living connection of the parts, the sympathy and reciprocity in a living organism, such as a class ought to be. In teaching, the first thing is to awaken the pupils: sometimes this can be done by persuasion—as Montaigne was awakened in the morning, when a boy, by music; more frequently it is by a rousing call, as by a trumpet; most commonly it is by the stir of companions. When a class is roused into activity, the members get fully as much benefit from one another, each one drawing or pushing his neighbor, as from the teacher, whose highest business will be to keep up the unity and the life. The coldest and hardest objects may be made to strike fire by collision. Davy melted two pieces of ice by rubbing them against each other; and the coldest and most obstinate natures may get fire and diffuse heat by being kept by the impetus of a lively teacher in constant molecular motion. The Rev. Mr. Pattison, speaking of Oxford, says: "In respect of seventy per cent. of its students, it is idle, hopelessly and incorrigibly idle."* There is no such lamentable disproportion, as I can testify, in those who receive ben-

---

* Another defect of the tutorial system is graphically described by Mr. Pattison: "Philosophy is taught not by professors who have given a life to the mastery of some one of the branches of moral or political science, but by young tutors. He is often too young to have had the time to study. He never will obtain the time, for his business as tutor is conceived to be to push his men through the portals of some examination which is awaiting them. Accordingly, he reads in his vacation, or in such moments of leisure as he can snatch, the last new book on the subject. He becomes, of course, an immediate convert to the theory of the latest speculator; he retails the same in his lectures, recommending it, perhaps, by eloquence and learning all his own, and when he becomes examiner, he examines on it." This candid passage lets us into the secret of the tendency towards German idealism and rationalism, which appeared in Oxford and Cambridge in the last age, and the degradation towards Comtism and materialism in the present age.

efit in Scotland and in the Irish Colleges, and this arises very much from the stimulus given by class lectures.

On the other hand, there is a risk that, in a large class, a great many, the cunning, the dull, and the idle, escape in the crowd; and the copious matter poured forth by the professor is apt to be like those gushing torrents of rain shower, which run off immediately into the rivers and the sea, without sinking into the soil to fertilize it. It is evident that a skillful tutor, taking up an individual pupil, can make him acquire a minute accuracy, so preferable to the vagueness and looseness with which so many content themselves in a promiscuous class. We are thus shut up to the conclusion, that in a perfect method, there should be a judicious combination of the two.* The lecture must be continued to give large general views, and communicate a stimulus, as by an electric current, to the whole class. But, then, there must be rigid examinations, from week to week, almost from day to day, to make the pupils "chew and digest," as Bacon expresses it, the food; and that the teacher may know to impart instruction in the measure that they are able to receive it. With the lecture, which can only be heard once, and if lost on that one occasion, is lost forever, there should be text-books, on which the stu-

---

* I may be allowed to state, that, in my two regular classes of logic and metaphysics, in Queen's College, I devoted one half the time to the delivery of elaborate lectures, and the other half to examination on these lectures, and on text-books, and to the criticism of essays. But I had also an Honor Class for higher logic and the history of philosophy, attended by those who had a special taste for the study.

dent may turn back once and again, as may suit his capacity and convenience. I hold that every professor should have not only a large general class, to which he gives an impetus by lecturing, he should have a small class of those who lag behind to be taught by an assistant, and also a select class taught by himself, and composed of the few who are to be made thoroughly masters of the subject, or engage in independent research. I am most anxious to see whether the American method, with its combined lectures and recitations, does or does not supply and unite these requisites.

IV.—WHAT IS THE PLACE AND THE VALUE OF EXAMINATIONS?

I refer now not to class-examinations or recitations which ought to be weekly, almost daily, but to general College-examinations on courses gone over or on subjects prescribed. These occupy a very important place in European Universities. A " first " and a " double first " class in Oxford, a place as a " wrangler " in Cambridge, are obtained by examinations, and upon these the valuable money fellowships depend. The fellowships in Dublin, which are of great value, are gained directly by competitive examinations. The honors and the scholarships of the Queen's University and Queen's Colleges are determined in the same manner. Of late years the Scottish Colleges have been copying from the English ones; on this point, I believe greatly to their advantage. In Germany there are no ordinary

Class or College examinations, but at the close, the students are examined by bureaus in order to their entrance on any office, ecclesiastical or civil.

Some people think that in certain of these Colleges there is too much of official and grading examination, and that the aim of the teaching is not to improve the mind, or even to convey a mastery of the subject, but simply so to drill that the result may appear in the answers; and the impression left is that subjects and studies are valued not for their own intrinsic value, but as they come out in the examinations. It is certain that the examinations may come so often as to interrupt the course of study or bring it to a premature conclusion—in short the plant may be kept from growing by fumbling too often about its roots to see if it is making progress. Then there is the evil of *cram*, in which an immense mass of food is taken at once, without the possibility of digesting it, and with all the evil of a surfeit. I have been told by young men, who have made up a science in a month or two for an examination, that they have lost it as speedily as they gained it, and have retained little else than an aversion to the study. It is certain that the preparation for an examination and a successful competition can never serve the purpose accomplished by a College residence: by well-cooked food being served up from day to day; by sitting habitually under a teacher competent for his work, and interested in it; by constant intercourse and interchange of thought with fellow-students; by recourse to well-furnished libraries and museums, and by the stimulus of College societies. The London University is now a mere examining body, giving degrees to all who can stand a trial on the subjects prescribed. I have no objection that there should be one such University to meet the case of those diligent youths who can not find it possible to attend a College course. But I should deplore to find the other Universities of the country reduced to the same level—when an attempt was made to turn the Queen's University into an examining board we successfully resisted the attempt. We must beware of making learning appear in the view of youth with the fixed passive gaze of the Egyptian Sphinx; we must seek to make it wear the life and the play of the Grecian Apollo. In a properly regulated course of study there must be leisure for rest and refreshing, for occasional promiscuous reading, and for rumination on the past, and for looking into the future. The student character and solid scholarship are to be formed, as the crust of the earth has been, by continual deposits building up layer upon layer; and the competitive examinations are to come in at the close, like the upheaving forces of the earth, to consolidate what is scattered as sand, and to uplift it and expose it to the view.

You see what is the view I take of examinations. I object to their being made a substitute for College residence, College attendance and training, which are of more value than any competitive trials. They are the folding and sealing of the document, which, however, in order to fulfil any purpose must first have been written out. But then they do serve a most important end when they come in to complete a collegiate course, shorter or longer. They then wind up the previous studies; they necessitate a revision of the whole; they bring every route to a point, and thus show us the connections of the studies gone over separately. It is a matter of fact that there is always more of accuracy of scholarship, and mastery of detail in those Colleges, in which there are careful revising examinations, than in those, in which there are merely loose lecturing and daily recitations. And there is no other way of determining fitness for graduation, for scholarships and for fellowships, than by some sort of competition, in which examinations must constitute the main element, always it may be with essays and original research.

V. WHAT ENCOURAGEMENT SHOULD BE GIVEN TO COLLEGIATE SCHOLARSHIP.

In many of the Colleges of Europe immense sums are expended every year in prizes, scholarships and fellowships. In Oxford there are eighty scholarships, of the average value of £65, open to competition every year on the part of undergraduate students; and for those, who have taken the degree, there are three hundred fellowships, worth about £300 a year each; the whole amounting to £90,000, and some twenty or thirty of these fall vacant annually. In the Queen's

Colleges £1500 a year is set apart in each for scholarships; and there are large money honors to be obtained by competition at the examinations of the Queen's University. The scholarships and fellowships, connected with the University of Edinburgh, are especially worthy of being looked to by the friends of higher education in America, inasmuch as they have all been supplied by private benevolence, and within the last few years. I will not specify those allocated to junior students, but it may be useful to refer to those reserved for graduates or advanced students. There is the Mackenzie Scholarship worth £120 a year, gained by eminence in classical and English literature, and tenable for four years. There is a Greek Travelling Scholarship, tenable for one year, and worth £70. There are four Baxter Scholarships, each worth £60 a year, and tenable for not more than four years; one for the best answering in mathematics, the second for the best answering in mental philosophy, the third for the best answering in physics, and the fourth in natural history. The Drummond Scholarship is worth £100 a year, and is tenable for three years; it is devoted to mathematics. There are three Tyndal Bruce Scholarships, each worth £100 a year, and tenable for three years; one for general scholarship, a second for philosophical and a third for Mathematical Scholarship. There is the Guthrie Fellowship devoted to classical literature, worth £100 a year, and tenable for four years; and the Hamilton Fellowship, allocated to logic, metaphysics and moral philosophy, of the value of

£100 a year, and continued for three years; and the Classical Fellowship with £100, and tenable for three years. There are scholarships in divinity and medicine, which I pass over—to refer only to the Swiney Lectureship in Geology, worth £144; and tenable for five years. Besides these endowments confined to Edinburgh, there are others open to the graduates of any Scottish University; thus there are three Ferguson Scholarships, of £80 each, devoted respectively to classics, mathematics and mental science; and the Shaw Fellowship in mental philosophy, worth £160, and tenable for two years. It is acknowledged on all hands that an immense impulse has been given to learning by these munificent foundations.

In such American Colleges as Princeton, the average answering at graduation, is quite equal, I believe, to that of the best of the European Universities.* But I rather think that there are a select few in several British and German Universities, who go beyond what has been attained on this side the Atlantic. And, I believe, that this has been effected very much by the encouragement given to higher scholarship on the part of the students. Is there no way by which you Americans, while retaining all your present excellencies, may acquire what others

---

* I am surprised to find Mr. Pattison (*Academical Organization*, p 150) saying, "In America scientific culture has never been introduced. It has no Universities, such as we understand by the term; the institutions so called being merely places for granting titular degrees." He refers in proof to the course of studies in Yale University—a course which seems to me to be a very good one.

have gained? This, I believe, could be accomplished by providing some sort of higher Scholarships or Fellowships as a reward of diligence and success in the past; and obliging those who accept them to continue their studies after graduation under the superintendence of the College. The grand hindrance to higher learning in the Colleges here is to be found in the circumstance that the best students, after getting their degree, rush at once into professional pursuits, and make no farther progress, if indeed they do not lose what they have so laboriously acquired. The friends of the American Colleges could not benefit them so effectually as by providing that those who have taste and talent for higher scholarship, should have an inducement to continue their studies after graduation as having a means of sustaining themselves while they do so. These distinguished alumni should be required to pursue special lines of study or to travel; and might be encouraged to produce the results in brief courses of lectures, delivered under the sanction of the College, and sure to be appreciated by the students.

There is another way in which the interests of education have been much promoted both in Prussia and Great Britain, and that is by Government patronage bestowed on those who succeed at public examinations. In Prussia, young men can enter the learned professions of law, medicine and the church only through the Universities and an examination. Not only so, but in order to entrance on the civil service of the country, an attendance at a gymnasium or University, followed by a rigid examination, is required. In Great Britain, all young men entering the public service, military, medical, or civil, down to tidewaiters and office porters, must submit to a literary examination. In many, offices such as the Royal Engineers and the Medical and Civil Service of India are to be had in this way and in no other. Some of the most valuable public offices in the world are gained in this way, such as the civil offices of India, which begin with £400 or £500 a year, and speedily rise to £1000, or possibly £1500, open to all young men. I am far from saying that this mode of appointment to Government employment is not liable to theoretical objections; but practically it is found to be vastly preferable to the old method, which proceeded by nepotism, or by political partisanship, in which the Member of Parliament was obliged to recommend the youth, who was pressed upon him by his supporters in his county or borough. There is, of course, always a risk of failure in the case of the appointment of untried young men; but when it depends on the success at a severe competitive trial in the higher branches, there is a security that the youth must possess good abilities; that he has a power of application and perseverance; and that he has not spent his time in indolence or vice—which last capacity or incapacity was sometimes reckoned as constituting his aptitude for the situation—those, unfit for anything else, being often foisted into a government office, when their friends happened to have influence with the dominant party. It is surely worthy of consideration, whether the offices in this country, requiring to be filled by young men, might not with advantage to the community, and to the great encouragement of learning, be thrown open to public competition instead of being determined by political partisanship.

VI. SHOULD THERE BE UNIVERSITY EXTENSION?

This is a question, which requires to be agitated in some parts of Europe. The German speaking nations, with their fifty-eight universities and nineteen thousand students, do not seem to stand in need of such extension; nor does Scotland, with its four old efficient universities; nor Ireland with its two universities, and its four state-endowed and its various denominational Colleges. But England certainly has much need of the establishment of new Colleges, especially in its great centres of wealth and population, such as London, and Manchester, and Bristol, and Newcastle.

Every friend of education and of mankind will rejoice to see Colleges extending all over this country; from the Atlantic to the Pacific, from Maine to New Mexico; advancing with the population of the country, refining its energy, and purifying its wealth. But we have a right to ask that, while new Universities are encouraged, the old be not discouraged. I believe that the excessive multiplication of small and ill-sustained Colleges in a district may be an enormous evil. In these days of rapid locomotion it is of little moment to a student, whether he have to go ten or twenty miles to a College, one hundred miles or five hundred. I believe that there is always more of stimulus, more of success, more of life, less of conceit, less of narrowness, of sectarianism, of knottiness, in large classes and large Colleges than in small ones. Care should certainly be taken that, in the excessive competition, the food do not become adulterated; that the new Colleges do not drag down the old till all sink to a Dead Sea level. We should rather strive that the old be bringing up the new to a higher standard; and that we have a number of Colleges thoroughly equipped by able men, by extensive apparatus, and by chairs for teaching every high branch of literature and science. We must not yield to the temptation, to which we are exposed, of sending unripe fruit into the market: or, to vary the metaphor, of resting contented with *lumber* fabrics. In new and waste countries they must be satisfied, and we do not blame them, with the log cabin; but then they rise as speedily as possible to the frame house; and as the country becomes older they would have the more solid brick and the stone; and now not only your capitols, but not a few of your private dwellings, are of marble. There ought to be such an ascension in your Colleges as the country grows older and richer: in the far West they may start with little better than our High Schools; but in the older East we must not rest satisfied till we have institutions to rival the grand old Universities of Europe, such as Oxford. and Cambridge, and Berlin, and Edinburgh.

What makes Oxford and Cambridge have such an influence on those who live within their walls, and which is sensibly felt even by those who pay them only a passing visit? The great men who have been there, and who still seem to look down upon us; the living men, not unworthy of them, and who are pointed out to us, as they walk through the courts; the talk of the tripos and the first class, and the double first and the wranglerships; the quiet life in the Colleges, and the active life in the examination halls, in the societies and the great University meetings; the manuscripts, the old books, the museums, all these create an academic atmosphere, in which it is bracing to breathe, and is felt to be more stimulating than all the excellent teaching of the tutors. Will our numerous friends not join with the professors and students in striving to create such an atmosphere here in Princeton, where we have grand names in the past, and need only like men in the present: by accessions to our apparatus and our library, and encouragements to the students to go on to the higher learning; and by the founding of new chairs of literature and science to make our College as adapted to these times as our forefathers made it suitable to their day?

For the handsome and considerate kindness shown by those who have so endeared themselves to me, as well as benefited this College, by endowing the presidential office, and furnishing me with a comfortable home, I here give public and hearty thanks. My personal comforts being provided for, I am free to look to other interests. Of late years, certain generous benefactors have endowed chairs in the College, and now we have a princely merchant devoting a large sum to its extension generally, and a well-known friend of science aims at placing on our height, with its wide horizon, the finest observatory in the world. They will be followed, I trust, by others. The friends of Princeton must come forward at this time to uphold her, and make her worthy of her ancient reputation, and enable her to advance with the times: one whom God has blessed, increasing the salaries of our hard-working and underpaid professors, who should be set free from drudgery and worldly anxieties to give a portion of their energy to the furtherance of learning and science; a second, by providing further accommodation for our students, that we may receive and house comfortably all who apply; a third by erecting a gymnasium for the bracing of the bodily frame;* a fourth, by enlarging our library or scientific apparatus; a fifth, by founding a scholarship, or junior fellowship for the encouragement of letters and high merit among students; and a sixth, by founding a new chair required by the progress of knowledge: we have scope here for every man's tastes and predilections.

Speaking of the desirableness of elevating the learning in our higher institutions, I have sometimes thought that, as Oxford University combines some

---

* Immediately after the Inauguration, two gentlemen subscribed $10,000 each, for the erection of a gymnasium.

twenty-two Colleges, and Cambridge eighteen, so there might in this country be a combination of Colleges in one University. Let every State have one University to unite all its Colleges, and appointing examiners and bestowing honors of considerable pecuniary value on more deserving students. Some such a combination as this, while it would promote a wholesome rivalry among the Colleges, would, at the same time, keep up the standard of erudition. Another benefit would arise: the examination of the candidates being conducted not by those who taught them, but by elected examiners, would give a high and catholic tone to the teaching in the Colleges. I throw out the idea that thinking men may ponder it.

But returning to ourselves. New Jersey College has a great prestige, second, I believe, to no other in the United States. But we cannot live on our past reputation—any more than our frames can be sustained on the food which we have partaken days ago. In these times, when it is known that all things move, earth and sun, stars and constellations, we cannot stop or remain stationary, except at the risk of being thrown out of our sphere, without the power of returning to it. In this new country, we have to look to our children more than our fathers, and "instead of the fathers shall be the children." You will have seen from the whole train of these observations, that I aim at keeping up the academic standard at Princeton. I have not torn myself from my native land and friends to be the mere head of a Mechanics' Institute; I would rather you should send me back to my old country at once than make me and your College submit to such humiliation. This College will repay the debt which it owes to the country not in a depreciated currency, but in the genuine coin, with the flying eagle upon it and the golden ring. Parents and guardians sending their sons to this venerable institution must have a security that they will receive as high an education as any College in this country—as any College in any country can furnish.

VII.—WHAT PLACE SHOULD RELIGION HAVE IN OUR COLLEGES?

In Scotland the Established Church long claimed an authority over the Colleges, and over all their teaching, and provided a form of religion. I can testify that it was little more than a form, and this not always the form of sound words. For years past the control of the Church of Scotland over any thing but the theological professors has been taken away, and with it all that remained of the form has disappeared: and now the Scottish Colleges profess to give nothing more than secular instruction, men of piety always seeking to imbue their whole teaching with a religious spirit. The keen battle being at present fought in England is likely to terminate in the same issue. But good men concerned about the religion and morality of young men cannot allow things to continue in that state. How, then, is religion to be grafted on State

Colleges open to all whatever their religious profession? I have thought much on this subject, and labored with some success to realize my idea in Belfast.* Let the State provide the secular instruction and the churches provide the religious training in the homes in which the students reside.

But, passing from foreign topics, this College has had a religious character in time past, and it will be my endeavor to see that it has the same in time to come. Religion should burn in the hearts, and shine, though they wis it not, from the face of the teachers; and it should have a living power in our meetings for worship, and should sanctify the air of the rooms in which the students reside. And in regard to religious truth, there will be no uncertain sound uttered within these walls. What is proclaimed here will be the old truth which has been from the beginning: which was shown in shadow in the Old Testament; which was exhibited fully in the New Testament as in a glass; which has been retained by the one Catholic Church in the darkest ages; which was long buried, but rose again at the Reformation;

---

* The Methodist body has spent £24,000 in erecting a fine College in the immediate neighborhood of Queen's College, Belfast. The students take the ordinary academic branches in Queen's College, and receive specially religious and theological instruction in their own College. The Irish Presbyterians have subscribed £3,000 for the erection of students' chambers attached to their Theological College, and open to all students intended for the ministry, whether in the Queen's College or the Theological College. I am convinced that it is in some such way as this that the churches are to provide religious instruction in connection with the State Colleges of Great Britain.

which was maintained by the grand old theologians of Germany, Switzerland, England, and Scotland; and is being defended with great logical power in the famous Theological Seminary with which this College is so closely associated. But over this massive and clearly-defined old form of sound words, I would place no theological doctor, not Augustine, not Luther, not Calvin, not Edwards, but another and far fairer face lifted up that it may draw all eyes towards it—"Jesus at once the author and the finisher of our faith." A religion of a neutral tint has nothing in it to attract the eye or the heart of the young or the old. I believe that the religion which can have any power in moving the minds and moulding the character of students or of others, must be the pure evangel of Jesus Christ.

But you will expect of one descended from the old Covenanting stock, who fought so resolutely for the rights of conscience, and whose blood dyed the heather hills of Scotland; from one who was brought up in a district where there are martyrs' tombs in every church-yard; from one who was connected for so many years with the Irish system of national education, which allows no one to tamper with the religious convictions of pupils, that he shall take care that every one here shall have full freedom of thought: that whatever be his religious creed or political party, be he from the North, or be he from the South, be he of a white or a dark color, he shall have free access to all the benefits which this college can bestow; and that a minority, nay, even a single conscientious individual, shall be protected from the tyranny of the majority, and encouraged to pursue his studies without molestation, provided always that not being interfered with himself, he does not interfere with others.

You have called me to the highest office, so I esteem it, which your great country could place at my disposal. But if I know my own heart, I am not vain, I am not even proud, as I might be, of the distinction conferred upon me. I am rather awed at the thought of the responsibility lying upon me. I come here, I find, amid high expectations, and how am I ever to come up to them? I get this College with a high reputation, and what if its lustre should diminish? My name is this day added to the roll which begins with Dickenson and Aaron Burr, embraces Jonathan Edwards, Davies, Finley, Witherspoon, Smith, Green, Carnahan, who have left their impress not only on this College, but on their country and times, and comes to one, who for long years felt so deep an interest in the welfare of the students, who was able to teach nearly every department in the institution over which he presided, and whom we will all delight to honor as he passes his remaining days in peace among us. Of a king in Israel it is said, that they buried him in the city, "but they brought him not into the sepulchres of the kings of Israel." I confess I should like, when my work is finished, to be buried among these kings in the realms of thought, that my dust may mingle with their dust, and my spirit mount to pure and eternal communion with them in heaven. I feel that the labor meanwhile will be congenial to me; my whole past life as a student, as a minister, and as a professor, should prepare me for it. My tastes have ever led me towards intercourse with young men. I have the same estimate of youth that the Spartans had, when Antipater demanded of them fifty youths as hostages, they answered, they would rather give twice the number of grown men. I rejoice that my lot calls me to labor among young men. I wish to enter into their feelings, to sympathize with them in their difficulties—with their doubts in these days of criticism, to help them in their fights, and rejoice with them in their triumphs. And so I devote my life, any gifts which God has given me, my experience as a minister of religion in a great era in the history of Scotland, my experience as a professor in a young and living College, under God to you and your service.

DR. McCOSH'S WORKS.

I.

THE METHOD OF DIVINE GOVERNMENT, PHYSICAL AND MORAL. 8vo. $2.50.

II.

TYPICAL FORMS AND SPECIAL ENDS IN CREATION. 8vo. $2.50.

III.

THE INTUITIONS OF THE MIND INDUCTIVELY INVESTIGATED. 8vo. $3.

IV.

AN EXAMINATION OF MR. J. S. MILLS' PHILOSOPHY; BEING A DEFENCE OF FUNDAMENTAL TRUTH. 8vo. $3.

V.

PHILOSOPHICAL PAPERS. Flexible cloth. $1.

ROBERT CARTER & BROTHERS,

530 BROADWAY, NEW YORK.

www.ingramcontent.com/pod-product-compliance
Lightning Source LLC
Chambersburg PA
CBHW032244080426
42735CB00008B/1000